# Common Formative Assessments
## for
## English Language Learners

# Common Formative Assessments
## for
## English Language Learners

Rachel Carrillo Syrja

LEAD+
LEARN
PRESS

ENGLEWOOD, COLORADO

The Leadership and Learning Center
317 Inverness Way South, Suite 150
Englewood, Colorado 80112
Phone 1.866.399.6019 | Fax 303.504.9417
www.LeadandLearn.com

Published by Lead + Learn Press, a division of Houghton Mifflin Harcourt.

Lead + Learn Press also publishes books in a variety of electronic formats. Some content that appears in print may not be available in electronic books.

Library of Congress Cataloging-in-Publication Data

Syrja, Rachel Carrillo, 1968-
 Common formative assessments for English language learners / Rachel Carrillo Syrja.
  p. cm.
 Includes bibliographical references and index.
 ISBN 978-1-935588-18-4 (alk. paper)
 1. English language—Study and teaching—Foreign speakers.  2. English language—
Ability testing.  I. Title.
 PE1128.A2S98 2012
 428.0071--dc23

                                                                                2011051936

ISBN 978-1-935588-18-4

Printed in the United States of America

16  15  14  13  12      01  02  03  04  05  06  07

# Contents

# List of Exhibits

# About the Author

**Rachel Carrillo Syrja**

Rachel Carrillo Syrja is a Professional Development Associate with The Leadership and Learning Center. During her 19 years in education, she has been a classroom teacher, mathematics coach and resource teacher, and professional developer. Her varied educational experiences as well as leadership roles have enhanced her knowledge and skills in the areas of curriculum, instruction, and assessment. Among her many leadership roles, she has designed and implemented district-wide staff development in the areas of English Language Development, working with struggling learners, standards-based education, and Assessment for Learning. Additionally, Rachel has conducted workshops for teachers and administrators on Data Teams, Professional Learning Communities (PLCs), and Using Assessment Data to Drive Instruction. She has also presented at national conferences such as ASCD. In addition, she is the author of *How to Reach and Teach English Language Learners.*

Raised in a bilingual household, Rachel has an acute sense of the needs of the English language learner. Working in a district that had a large population of English learners and Title I students, Rachel placed a strong emphasis on serving these groups in all of her endeavors. While in her own district, she worked on implementing a stronger ESL program district-wide by synthesizing state data and district data to build a comprehensive program that addressed the needs of ELLs at their individual language development levels. She facilitated a district-level PLC to formulate and implement solutions for this complex and timely issue.

Rachel earned her B.S. from Occidental College in Los Angeles, California, and her master's degree in Educational Administration and Administrative Services Credential from Point Loma University in San Diego, California.

Rachel resides in Pomona, California. She enjoys reading, traveling, writing, and spending time with her family.

# Introduction

While Sir Isaac Newton's quote reminds us of the promise of education, sadly that promise seems untenable to many English language learners (ELLs) in the United States. While they show up every day in classrooms across this country, access to core academic content proves illusory to them, at best. I was one of those children. Armed with nothing more than the alphabet song I'd memorized from *Sesame Street*, I showed up to school every day eager to understand even the slightest bit of English. My parents unequivocally subscribed to the idea that with an education, anything was possible. It was precisely that idea that saw me through even the most challenging times.

I am quite certain that there is no teacher who intentionally sets out to exclude a whole segment of her class from high-quality, differentiated instruction and assessments, yet every day countless numbers of English learners sit in classrooms where they are neither accessing the content nor being assessed in a way that would assist their teachers in helping them to access that content. In fact, as long as teaching and assessing English learners remains a mystery, we will continue to see the same achievement gaps that have defined the educational experience for so many English learners.

While it has long been established by such experts in the field as Rick Stiggins, James Popham, and Larry Ainsworth that assessment is an integral part of the learning process, the complex process of assessing English learners has never been clearly defined for educators. The process has remained a mystery with few resources made available to help educators with the actual development of high-quality assessments, formative and summative. I hear the same request from teachers coast to coast: "I know that I need to assess my English learners' content and language proficiency, but *HOW* do I do it?" What is needed is a proven process for the development and refining of high-quality assessments for English learners. On the following pages, teachers will find a process to follow, whether they are English as a Second Language teachers, or content area or mainstream teachers.

In their article on equitable assessment practices for English learners, Mark LaCelle-Peterson and Charlene Rivera argue that assessment—the gathering and interpreting of information about students' knowledge or achievement in relation to a standard—must be appropriate for the learners being assessed (1994). In the 1990s, as we approached the age of standards and accountability in public schools, LaCelle-Peterson and Rivera reflected upon the inappropriate methods of assessing English learners that plagued classrooms across the nation at that time. They warned of the assumption that assessment practices and curricular innovations that contributed to the success of monolingual students would also work for ELLs. While we like to think that with time comes progress, the absence of tools and strategies for teachers to accomplish this intensive process has meant that many still hold true to this fallacy. The chapters that follow will challenge that notion and instead present teachers with a process and model for developing differentiated assessments that meet the needs of ELLs.

# CHAPTER 1
# The English Language Learner

Recent demographic data confirms that the number of immigrant students in the United States who have limited English proficiency is growing exponentially. Not surprisingly, students who are learning English as a second language are the fastest-growing segment of the school-age population. Sadly, although the number of English language learners (ELLs) nationwide has increased, their academic achievement continues to lag far behind that of their native English-speaking peers.

Examples abound across the country. A policy brief by Professor Jamal Abedi and Ron Dietel of UCLA examines this widening achievement gap in several districts across the country since the inception of the No Child Left Behind (NCLB) legislation (Abedi and Dietel, 2004). In Boston Public Schools, the largest district in the state of Massachusetts, with a population of approximately 10 percent ELL students, the ELL gap grew from 11 percentage points in 1998 to 20 percentage points in 2003. Abedi and Dietel postulate that rapid progress by students overall combined with policies that test ELL students who have lived in the United States for very short periods of time contribute to a growing ELL achievement gap in many states and school districts. In 2003, for example, all ELL students in Massachusetts were required to participate in Massachusetts Comprehensive Assessment System (MCAS) testing in English. While it certainly makes sense to expect English learners to participate in state testing after reaching a certain level of English proficiency, requiring students who have limited English skills to participate in an assessment for which they are ill equipped appears unfair and serves no practical purpose.

While assessing students in a language they are not proficient in is one contributing factor to the widening achievement gap, a second factor lies hidden within the subgroup itself. When English learners become proficient in English language arts, they are no longer classified as ELLs and are thus no longer included in the results. Removing the proficient students from the subgroup naturally lowers average scores, as does the arrival of newcomers with limited English. This creates a "treadmill" effect in which the subgroup as a whole can never make much progress even if individuals do.

This is a phenomenon unique to English learner status and one that has not been widely understood. In essence, when comparing the number of students proficient from one year to another, it is likely that the highest-performing English learners from the previous year are no longer included in the present year's results but have instead been replaced by newcomer English learners who make the achievement gap appear even wider. Just being aware of this fact can help educators make informed instructional decisions for English learners. This awareness is also essential for policy-makers when making broad decisions based on data that can be misleading.

## DEMOGRAPHIC TRENDS

### The Impact of Recent Immigration

The populations of elementary and secondary schools across the country continue to change as a result of record-high numbers of immigrants entering the country. Between 1970 and 2000, the number of school-age children of immigrants grew from 6 percent to 19 percent. The 1990s saw the number of children of immigrants grow more than 72 percent in secondary schools and 39 percent in elementary schools. This high rate of growth is particularly significant because many secondary schools are not yet structured to promote language acquisition and content-area mastery designed specifically for newcomers (Ruíz-de-Velasco and Fix, 2000). It is fair to say that these schools are equally unprepared to assess content proficiency for a student with limited language abilities. While the subject of this book is assessing content proficiency for students with limited English proficiency, the topic of assessing the progress of students in their acquisition of English will also be addressed. Content teachers will want to examine the portions of the book dedicated specifically to the creation of differentiated content assessments, while teachers of English as a Second Language (ESL) will want to also examine the portions of the book focused on assessing language acquisition.

### A Growing English Learner Population

Along with a growing number of immigrants, the population of ELLs has also grown dramatically in the last 20 years. Between 1993 and 2003, the ELL population grew by 84 percent, while the overall student population rose 12 percent. The number of ELLs in elementary schools from 1980 to 2000 increased from 5 to 7 percent, while in secondary schools the number of ELLs increased from 3 to 5 percent.

While the population of immigrants has increased for states with traditionally high numbers of ELLs, it has also increased dramatically for many states that have not traditionally had high numbers of ELLs. The states that have experienced the largest increases in the last decade are included in the following chart.

| State | ELL Population Growth Rate |
|---|---|
| Nevada | 206% |
| North Carolina | 153% |
| Georgia | 148% |
| Nebraska | 125% |

These increases have especially affected the large urban centers in these states, such as Las Vegas, Nevada; Charlotte, North Carolina; Atlanta, Georgia; and Omaha, Nebraska. The data shows that ELLs are highly concentrated in a few urban schools that are also highly minority, low income, and disproportionately likely to fail federal standards (Capps, et al., 2005). In areas that are newly experiencing an influx of ELLs, the burden is often overwhelming as these areas often lack the resources and appropriately credentialed teachers to meet the needs of so many students. Such demographic trends have, not surprisingly, led to a crisis in educating ELLs.

## Characteristics of the Current English Learner Population

Demographic trends show that after English, Spanish is the most widely used language in the United States. While it is estimated that approximately 20 percent of school-age children speak a language other than English, 14 to 16 percent of them speak Spanish as their primary language at home, while the remaining 4 to 6 percent speak a language other than Spanish (Reyes and Moll, 2004). The majority of the K–5 population of English language learners, 76 percent, speak Spanish and are of Latino/Hispanic background (Capps, et al., 2004).

The Early Childhood Longitudinal Study of Kindergarten Children (ECLS-K) of 1998, a national study that looked at more than 22,000 students who were about to enter kindergarten, found that 68 percent of the children were classified as native English speakers, while 18 percent were classified as language minority (LM) (Espinosa, Laffey, and Whittaker, 2006). About 13 percent of the total sample were classified as Spanish speaking, 2.7 percent were identified as Asian speaking, and 2 percent spoke a European language. The majority of these language-minority students (52 percent) lived in high levels of poverty, but, strikingly, 80 percent of the Spanish speakers who were initially identified as being the least fluent in English were in the lowest two socioeconomic status (SES) quintiles (Espinosa, Laffey, and

Whittaker, 2006). These data not only point to an increasingly diverse population, but also clearly show that many incoming language-minority students, particularly Hispanic students, live in highly impoverished homes.

## EXAMINING WHAT WORKS WITH ENGLISH LEARNERS

In 1997, research conducted by Virginia Collier and Wayne Thomas made the case for conducting long-term research into what works for ELLs (Thomas and Collier, 1997). The urgency of that study is just as significant today as it was 14 years ago. While books such as *Classroom Instruction that Works with English Language Learners* by Jane D. Hill and Kathleen M. Flynn have contributed greatly to our repertoire for what works, educators still lack specific strategies for different levels of English language acquisition and especially lack resources for effective formative assessment strategies for ELLs (Hill and Flynn, 2006). In the same study, Collier and Thomas also state that long-term studies into program efficacy for ELLs need to be undertaken. In fact, their findings show that while in the short term some programs show promising results, these very programs prove detrimental in the later years of an ELL's educational career (Thomas and Collier, 1997, p.14). For example, while ELLs who are mainstreamed into English-only programs in the early elementary years may show initial success, those advances are often short lived when content becomes much more complex in the middle and high school years and these same students begin to struggle because they lack the academic vocabulary to be successful. Sadly, high failure rates for these students often result in many of them dropping out of a system that has not served them well.

## FACTORS AFFECTING THE ACQUISITION OF LANGUAGE

The path to English proficiency is a long and bumpy one—oftentimes fraught with numerous challenges. In spite of that fact, research in the area of second-language acquisition has helped us identify the conditions under which most students can successfully learn English. One thing is clear: the rate at which a child acquires a second language is dependent upon several factors, with the most significant factor being the amount of formal schooling the child had in his primary language. The most comprehensive study we have on the acquisition of language is the longitudinal study conducted by Wayne Thomas and Virginia Collier from 1982 to 1996. In that study, Thomas and Collier looked at the language acquisition of 700,000 students. They considered factors ranging from socioeconomic status to number of years of primary-language schooling. Of all the factors considered, the amount of formal schooling a child received prior to arriving in U.S. schools outweighed all other variables (Thomas and Collier, 1997, p. 14). Other key findings from their studies include the following:

- Students between the ages of eight and 11 who had two to three years of formal schooling in their native language took five to seven years to test at grade level in English.

- Conversely, students with little or no formal schooling in their native language who arrived before the age of eight took seven to 10 years to test at grade level in English.

- Students who were below grade level in their native language also took between seven and 10 years to reach just the 50th percentile, and many of them never reached grade-level proficiency. (Thomas and Collier, 1997)

James Cummins' research corroborates these findings. His studies found that a significant level of fluency in conversational language, Basic Interpersonal Communication Skills (BICS), can be achieved in two to three years. However, to reach near-native proficiency levels in the academic language, or Cognitive Academic Language Proficiency (CALP), requires between five and seven years (1996).

We see this evidenced in classrooms every day when we hear our English learners conversing beautifully in English and are misled to believe that the fact that they "sound fluent" translates into academic fluency. We are left exasperated when these same students fail to complete classroom or homework assignments, particularly if the assignments involve reading and writing. What we've failed to understand is that while these students may have mastered interpersonal communication skills (BICS), they have not yet mastered the cognitive language necessary for completing many of the assignments and tasks required of all students. So while we may think that these students are being lazy or disengaged, the real issue lies in the fact that the assignments are not appropriate to the students' true levels of language acquisition.

## THREE MAJOR CHALLENGES

While demographic changes have presented states and districts that have not historically had high ELL populations with some incredible obstacles, states that have traditionally had high levels of ELLs face challenges of their own. Nationally, three particular challenges point to an evolving crisis in the education of English language learners.

The first of these challenges comes indirectly from the implementation of the No Child Left Behind Act of 2002. Within that legislation, Title I and Title III contain provisions that specifically address ELLs. Title I requires schools to improve the performance of ELLs on state assessments in the areas of reading and math. Title I also establishes that ELLs are a protected subgroup along with other racial and ethnic groups, and as such requires schools to report their assessment results annually. Schools that do not meet the performance targets face restructuring and eventually possible school closure.

Title III requires schools to measure and improve ELLs' language proficiency. It also holds states accountable for the improvement in language proficiency of ELLs on an annual basis and provides support for states and school districts to create new assessments of language proficiency (Capps, et al., 2005). Title III establishes three annual measurable achievement objectives (AMAOs) that all teachers who work with English learners should be aware of:

- **AMAO 1** establishes annual increases in the number or percentage of children making progress in learning English. In essence, this AMAO requires that ELLs make a one-level improvement in language proficiency each year. For example, if they are classified as a Level 2, their language proficiency level should increase to a Level 3 by the end of the next school year.

- **AMAO 2** establishes annual increases in the number or percentage of children attaining English language proficiency (reclassification or redesignation) by the end of each school year.

- **AMAO 3** establishes adequate yearly progress (AYP) for ELLs in meeting grade-level academic achievement standards in English language arts and mathematics.

Mainstream teachers who do not teach ESL but who may have English learners in their classrooms may not even be familiar with AMAOs or with the growth targets that ELLs are expected to meet. So important are these growth targets to a school's ability to meet AYP requirements that all teachers of ELLs need to be aware of the AMAO growth targets that apply to them and should have an idea about how those targets impact their instruction.

The challenge to educators lies in the unexpected impact that these provisions in NCLB have had on the landscape of teaching ELLs. Due to the increased focus on rapid acquisition of English, many more states, led by California, are placing ELLs in English immersion or mainstream classes in which they receive little to no primary-language support and minimal ESL instruction. As expected, this trend has already proved to have negative repercussions on achievement for ELLs. English mainstream programs, otherwise known as submersion programs, have proliferated despite research that shows that students learn more when they are taught in a language they can understand and with materials that are comprehensible to them (Cummins, 1989; Krashen, 1981; McLaughlin, 1992; Ramírez, et al., 1991).

Studies on language learning by Thomas and Collier (1997) have confirmed that rapid acquisition has detrimental effects on the long-term success of ELLs. While students in English mainstream classes may initially appear to acquire English and reclassify more quickly, those gains quickly disappear when they reach middle and high school and the cognitive demands of school increase dramatically. When they do reach this point, these students who have long been reclassified and are no longer receiving language support in the form of ESL begin to lag far behind their native English-speaking peers. They struggle to learn in their content-area classes and find that their investment in learning is no longer paying off. Graduation becomes an insurmountable goal, and many end up dropping out. Schools with high concentrations of second-language learners that experience increased dropout rates no longer meet graduation standards required under NCLB for ELLs and other students, thus perpetuating the achievement gap for English learners.

A second challenge appears when we closely analyze data from the 2000 census. The census revealed that over 75 percent of ELLs in elementary schools and over 50 percent of ELLs in secondary schools were born in the United States, and many of those students also had parents who were born in the United States (Capps, et al., 2005). While learning a second language is a complex process, research has shown that the typical student will take between seven and 10 years to progress through five predictable levels of acquisition (see Exhibit 1.1). However, after seven or more

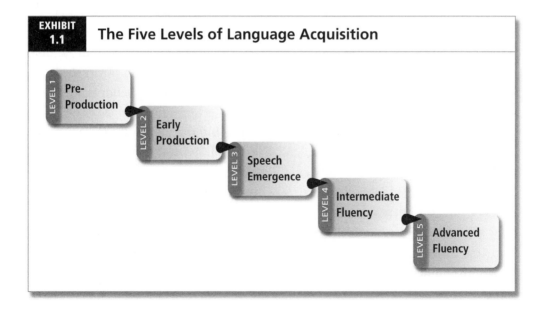

**EXHIBIT 1.1** **The Five Levels of Language Acquisition**

LEVEL 1 Pre-Production
LEVEL 2 Early Production
LEVEL 3 Speech Emergence
LEVEL 4 Intermediate Fluency
LEVEL 5 Advanced Fluency

years in school, these U.S.-born students have failed to become proficient in English. This data coupled with what we know about language acquisition leads us to conclude that the current educational approach for this particular group of ELLs has not proved successful.

A new acronym, LTELs, or Long-Term English Learners, has been coined to describe this group of students. LTELs are students who for a variety of reasons never reach proficiency in English. They are often referred to as students who are "stuck" at Level 3, Speech Emergence, of language proficiency and never reach Level 4 or 5, Intermediate or Advanced Fluency, and thus are never reclassified.

The third major challenge that has emerged from census data is the growing segregation of ELLs. We know from the demographic data that six states have the highest concentration of school-age immigrant children: California, New York, Texas, Florida, Illinois, and New Jersey. In California, almost 50 percent of all school-age children were children of immigrants (Capps, et al., 2005). In 1999, over 53 percent of ELLs attended schools where more than 30 percent of all students were ELLs (De Cohen, Clemencia, and Clewell, 2005). These trends indicate that ELLs are attending schools that are not only economically and ethnically segregated, but also linguistically isolated. Another disturbing fact is that these schools are disproportionately failing to meet state standards, and many are currently facing sanctions.

Unfortunately, this pattern is not one we see just in states with high immigrant populations. It is a pattern that is now also evident in states with small but growing immigrant populations.

Research from the Urban Institute has examined these schools with high ELL concentrations and found that they are typically larger than schools with few or no ELL students, and have less-experienced administrative and teaching staffs (De Cohen, Clemencia, and Clewell, 2005). In a study by the American Education Research Association (Cochran-Smith and Zeichner, 2006), showing the educational and community benefits of integrated schools for both white and minority students, the findings confirmed that segregated, predominantly minority schools offer profoundly unequal educational opportunities.

The children who attend these predominantly minority schools experience this inequality in several ways, including having less-qualified, less-experienced teachers, high levels of instability caused by a rapid teacher turnover rate, fewer educational resources, and limited exposure to peers who can serve as role models and positively influence their academic learning. These inequalities result in typical measures of educational outcomes, such as high school graduation rates and scores on standardized tests, being lower in schools with high percentages of nonwhite students (Cochran-Smith and Zeichner, 2006).

## STAGES OF LANGUAGE ACQUISITION

In 1983, Stephen Krashen and Tracy Terrell introduced us to the five stages of language acquisition. The stages are based upon the research of J. Cummins (1996) as well as Krashen and Terrell's own Natural Approach theory of language acquisition (1983).

**Level 1: Pre-Production** is the first stage of language acquisition and is sometimes referred to as the silent period. During this time, English learners are in a highly receptive state in which they are quietly observing and taking in the language around them. They may be able to nod yes or no in response to very basic questions and may also be able to gesture. This stage can last anywhere from zero to six months.

**Level 2: Early Production** is the second stage of language acquisition and is marked by a student making initial attempts at producing language. During this stage, the student begins to move from a highly receptive state to a productive state marked by the ability to begin responding with one- or two-word responses. Level 2 may last from six months to a year.

**Level 3: Speech Emergence** is the third stage of language acquisition. At this stage, the student has good comprehension and is producing an increasing amount of language. While the student may have acquired some academic language, the majority of the language the student can use and produce is basic interpersonal or social language. Level 3 may last somewhere between one and three years.

**Level 4: Intermediate Fluency**, the fourth stage of language acquisition, is attained when the student has excellent comprehension of both social and academic language. The student makes few grammatical errors and can answer questions that require more than a one-sentence response. Level 4 can last up to two years.

**Level 5: Advanced Fluency** is the final stage of language acquisition. At this stage, the student begins to approximate the language sophistication of a native English speaker. The focus at this stage is on learning the nuances of the English language. This final stage may last from one to two years.

While individual states have come up with their own levels of language acquisition, those levels have most likely been based upon these traditional levels. The language acquisition levels used throughout the book will be based upon these five research-based levels.

## KEY TERMINOLOGY—
## THE IMPORTANCE OF A COMMON LANGUAGE

It is critically important that schools and teams of teachers have a common language with which to discuss the elements of their program. Not possessing a common language can lead to misunderstanding and potential problems. This is particularly an issue when we look toward implementing an initiative yet don't possess a common understanding or definition of that initiative. For example, I have visited numerous school systems across the country in which I am assured that Professional Learning Communities (PLCs) have been implemented. When visiting teams of teachers in those buildings, I find that there are as many definitions of a PLC as there are teachers in the school, some of which are in direct contradiction to what the administration has defined as a PLC. Therefore, the first order of business for a school site that is beginning to implement common formative assessments for ELLs is ensuring that it has a common language and a common understanding of the terminology involved in the process. In the following paragraphs, I have listed some basic assessment terminology as well as terms that all adults who work with ELLs should possess.

**Common Formative Assessments**—Refers to more than just an "assessment in common." These are teacher-created assessments that are based upon a set of prioritized concepts and skills, the results of which are used collaboratively to determine next steps for learning in the instructional sequence for each student.

**English Language Learner (ELL)**—Refers to a student who has been identified as a limited English speaker when initially enrolled in our school system. It is important to remember that ELL refers to the student and *not* the program.

**Formative Assessment**—Refers to assessment *for* learning events that happen while the learning is taking place, the results of which are used to provide detailed feedback to students and teachers about how to improve achievement. Formative assessments and the results from these assessments help to promote greater learning and are highly motivating, particularly to low-achieving students.

**Heritage Language Speaker**—Refers to an individual who spoke or understood Spanish as a child but was never formally educated in Spanish. These students never learned the formal structures and patterns of the language well enough to be fluent in it.

**Limited English Proficient (LEP)**—A term initially used to describe the population of students now described as ELLs. The term LEP was replaced because it was considered to have negative connotations.

**Summative Assessment**—Refers to assessment *of* learning events that take place at the conclusion of learning, the results of which are used to assign grades and record mastery.

## ENGLISH LANGUAGE LEARNER PROGRAM OPTIONS

Program options for ELLs must be carefully planned and thought out by each individual school site. Considerations such as number of students, number of appropriately certified teachers, language background and prior schooling experience of our ELL population, and so on, must be taken into consideration when establishing viable program options for our students. It is not enough to merely say that your school or district has a dual immersion program—you will need to clearly define what that program looks like based on the resources available to you and on the specific needs of your language learner population. For example, it may not be feasible to offer a bilingual program if it cannot be fully implemented or implemented in a way that is educationally sound for your students. Whatever programs you may have, the important thing is to make sure that every teacher has a common definition and understanding of what that program looks like at your site. The following are some of the most common ELL program options.

**Bilingual Program.** The bilingual program develops primary-language (L1) literacy while simultaneously teaching English. There are two models of bilingual programs, **Early-Exit** and **Late-Exit**, with Late-Exit showing much greater rates of success. In an Early-Exit program, the primary language is used for about one-third of the time in kindergarten and first grade, with a rapid phase-out of the primary language happening by the end of first grade. By contrast, in a Late-Exit program primary language instruction begins in kindergarten, with increasing amounts of English instruction thereafter, up to approximately 60 percent in grades 5 and 6. The core subjects, such as language arts, math, social studies, and science, are taught in the primary language and, depending upon the type of bilingual program, English is introduced at varying rates. In addition to instruction in the core content areas, all students have a structured ESL or ELD (English Language Development) program that supports the teaching of the English language. When students reach cognitive proficiency in their primary language as well as Intermediate Fluency in English, they are gradually transitioned into English for the core subjects. According to the research findings of Thomas and Collier, the bilingual program, when implemented correctly, is perhaps one of the best options available for ELLs; that is, as long as the following conditions are met:

- The school has a cohesive, well organized bilingual program and can offer it to the student for as long as possible, at a minimum from kindergarten through fifth or sixth grade (Thomas and Collier, 1997, p.15).

- Students are provided with a minimum of 30 minutes daily of high-quality ESL or ELD instruction until they are reclassified and have reached fluency in English.

- The school is able to provide a highly qualified, fully credentialed bilingual teacher for each grade level, at least through fifth or sixth grade.

**Dual Immersion Program.** In some cases this type of program may also be referred to as bilingual immersion, dual language, developmental bilingual education, or two-way immersion. In a dual immersion program, every student is immersed in learning to speak two languages simultaneously. For example, the English language learners are maintaining their primary language while learning English, and English-only students are learning a second language (L2) while learning their regular content. The method for achieving this differs greatly, with some schools opting for the 50/50 split, with English accounting for 50 percent of the day and the L2 accounting for the remaining 50 percent. Regardless of the model used, the goal in this program is that all students exit the program being bilingual. Research on program efficacy has shown that along with the bilingual program, this is one of the most effective of all ELL program options (Thomas and Collier, 1997).

**English Immersion Program.** In this program, English learners receive a percentage of daily instruction in their primary language and a percentage in English. Typically, the minimum rate of L1 to L2 is a 50/50 split. Teachers in English immersion classrooms use primary language and sheltered instructional strategies to help ELLs fully access the core content. Successful implementation of English immersion is dependent on the same conditions being met as for bilingual programs (see description of the bilingual program in a previous paragraph). English immersion is also an effective program for ELLs.

**English Mainstream.** Technically, this is not considered an ELL program because it provides no primary-language support. However, currently states such as California, Arizona, and Massachusetts place the majority of their ELLs in mainstream classes (Gándara, Maxwell-Jolly, and Driscoll, 2005, p. 8). English mainstream programs place students in an English-only classroom and provide limited L1 support. English mainstream is often referred to as a "sink or swim" program. Long-term studies have found that while students in English mainstream programs are reclassified surprisingly quickly and do quite well in early elementary school, their long-term success is not as positive. In fact, once these students reach middle school and high school, they begin to lose much of the ground they had gained initially and are not able to sustain the gains made during the elementary school years (Thomas and Collier, 1997, p. 36). Many English learners in mainstream programs struggle tremendously to keep up with their English-only peers. For obvious reasons, English mainstream programs are not the best option for all ELLs.

**English as a Second Language or English Language Development (ESL/ELD).** All English language learners, regardless of their language program, should receive a minimal amount of ESL/ELD instruction. In most states and districts, ELLs receive a minimum of 45 minutes to an hour of ESL/ELD instruction per day. The instruction in these classes should focus on teaching the structures and patterns of the English language. ESL may be offered as either a pull-out or push-in program.

## INSTRUCTIONAL STRATEGIES

While there are numerous strategies that can be used with English learners, the following represent the two major categories of strategies that most of those strategies fall into. As with all students, teachers must carefully consider the needs of each English learner prior to identifying the appropriate strategy.

**Sheltered Instruction**. Also referred to as SDAIE, or Specially Designed Academic Instruction in English, in California. Both of these terms refer to a set of strategies used to teach core content to ELLs. These strategies help students access the content despite their limited proficiency in English. Research in language acquisition has shown that Level 3 ELLs and those at the higher levels benefit the most from the use of sheltered instructional strategies.

**Total Physical Response (TPR)**. TPR is a set of strategies that help ELLs in the beginning levels of language acquisition, Level 1 and Level 2, access the content. It was originally developed by James Asher in the 1970s. These strategies involve the use of commands, modeling, body movements, and gestures to establish communication in the very early stages of language acquisition. TPR is a very specific set of strategies that need to be implemented fully and with fidelity. Simply adding physical movements to your lessons does not make it TPR.

## CONCLUSION

The most important order of business for any school with English language learners is understanding the profiles of these students. In order to do this effectively, we must examine the demographic trends for our school or district over the last few years. Knowing the countries of origin of our students, the number of years of schooling they've had, and the educational levels of their parents are all significant pieces of information that all teachers who work with English learners should have access to. This does not mean just ESL teachers, but also content or self-contained mainstream teachers who have English learners in their classrooms. These are all facts that help shape the way we address the needs of our English language learners and their families.

Possessing a common language about ELLs and assessment types will help us to determine how common formative assessments fit into an integrated assessment system that begins with the content and language proficiency standards—all topics we will examine in more depth in Chapter 2.

## DISCUSSION QUESTIONS

1. Have we examined the recent demographic trends in our school/district? Do we have a linguistically isolated school population? If so, how are we ensuring that they are receiving the best opportunities for success?

2. Have we examined the unique characteristics of our English learner population? For example:

   What are the countries of origin and primary languages represented by our ELLs?

   Do we know how much prior schooling they've had?

   What is the educational background of their parents/families?

   Is it possible to create a database containing this information that can be shared with all teachers of English learners?

3. How are we making teachers aware of AMAOs?

4. Are ESL/ELD teachers made aware of AMAOs 1 and 2? Are English language arts and mathematics teachers aware of AMAO 3?

   AMAO 1: How many or what percentage of children are making progress in learning English?

   AMAO 2: How many or what percentage of children are attaining English language proficiency (reclassification or redesignation) by the end of each school year?

   AMAO 3: How many or what percentage of ELLs are meeting grade-level academic achievement standards in English language arts and mathematics? (Adequate Yearly Progress of the ELL subgroup in English language arts and mathematics?)

5. Have we examined our past performance in meeting AMAO growth targets? If we've had good performance, have we identified the practices that led to those results? If we have not met our growth targets, have we identified the practices that are not working?

6. Are we establishing an appropriate timeline for ELLs to acquire English (Late-Exit) or are we expecting ELLs to make a rapid progression through the different levels (Early-Exit)? If we have an Early-Exit program where our ELLs are quickly reclassified, how are we ensuring that they will continue to be successful through middle school and high school? What supports can we put in place to ensure that they receive timely support if and when they begin to struggle?

# CHAPTER 2

# The Big Picture: How Powerful Practices Connect for English Language Learners

"What works with English language learners?" It's a question that teachers of English learners grapple with constantly, but one for which frustratingly few answers exist. While we work tirelessly to meet the needs of all of the diverse learners in our classrooms, finding what works with English learners presents a formidable challenge to educational systems across the country. While our nation has seen a dramatic change in demographics over the last few years, with English learners becoming a significant subgroup in some unexpected locations, it seems the research on what works with English learners has not kept stride with the growth. In particular, educational systems find themselves lacking resources and strategies that work specifically with this subgroup.

What we do know works with all students are common formative assessments that teachers create and score, and that provide detailed feedback to both teachers and students. In fact, formative assessment has proved to be one of the most effective strategies teachers can use. We will look more closely at the impact of formative assessment in Chapter 3.

Most classroom teachers and schools have elaborate summative assessment systems (assessments *of* learning) in place that are designed to be used as accountability measures to help us determine the status of learning at the end of a learning cycle. However, most concede that the assessment system is not balanced and does not contain an equal number of high-quality formative assessments (assessments *for* learning) that are meant to promote greater learning and take place while the learning is happening. What we need, then, is balance—an assessment system that provides both high-quality assessments *of* learning that confirm learning, and well-aligned assessments *for* learning that provide students and teachers with feedback that can be used to promote even greater learning (Stiggins, et al., 2005).

Stiggins et al. (2005) describe the perfect assessment system as a set of doors that must literally be opened in a sequence. They stress that as a school system accomplishes the tasks within each door, they move closer to a perfect assessment system. Practically speaking, they encourage districts to establish their own priorities, starting places, and sequence for completing the work that needs to be done to implement a well-aligned assessment system. (See Exhibit 2.1.)

Similarly, Ainsworth and Viegut have developed the Standards-Assessment Alignment Diagram to graphically represent a comprehensive instruction and assessment system model as well as the deliberate alignment of each level of assessment with the ones that precede and follow it (2006). (See Exhibit 2.2.) Regardless of the process used, either of these models can be adapted for English language learners by using the language proficiency standards along with the content standards in each step of the process.

## THE ASSESSMENT AND INSTRUCTION SEQUENCE FOR ENGLISH LEARNERS

Both of these models highlight the major components of a comprehensive, standards-based instruction and assessment system. When developing an aligned assessment system for English learners, we must consider the following components:

1. Content standards and language proficiency standards

2. Priority standards

3. "Unwrapped" standards, Big Ideas, and Essential Questions

4. Common formative pre- and post-assessments, and summative assessments

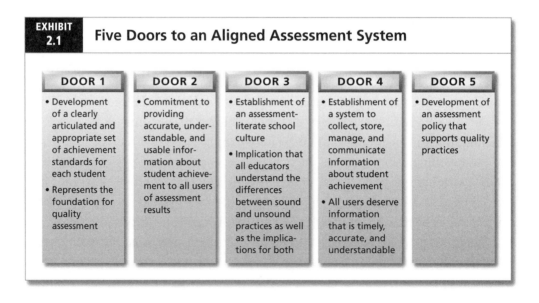

**EXHIBIT 2.1    Five Doors to an Aligned Assessment System**

| DOOR 1 | DOOR 2 | DOOR 3 | DOOR 4 | DOOR 5 |
|---|---|---|---|---|
| • Development of a clearly articulated and appropriate set of achievement standards for each student<br><br>• Represents the foundation for quality assessment | • Commitment to providing accurate, understandable, and usable information about student achievement to all users of assessment results | • Establishment of an assessment-literate school culture<br><br>• Implication that all educators understand the differences between sound and unsound practices as well as the implications for both | • Establishment of a system to collect, store, manage, and communicate information about student achievement<br><br>• All users deserve information that is timely, accurate, and understandable | • Development of an assessment policy that supports quality practices |

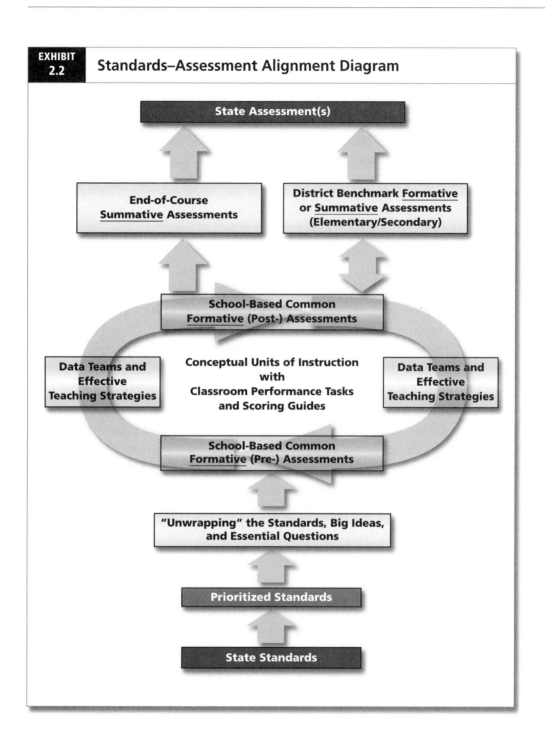

**EXHIBIT 2.2**

## Standards–Assessment Alignment Diagram

State Assessment(s)

End-of-Course Summative Assessments

District Benchmark Formative or Summative Assessments (Elementary/Secondary)

School-Based Common Formative (Post-) Assessments

Data Teams and Effective Teaching Strategies

Conceptual Units of Instruction with Classroom Performance Tasks and Scoring Guides

Data Teams and Effective Teaching Strategies

School-Based Common Formative (Pre-) Assessments

"Unwrapping" the Standards, Big Ideas, and Essential Questions

Prioritized Standards

State Standards

5. Instructional unit design, including classroom-differentiated performance assessments

6. Collaborative scoring of student work, including implications for differentiated grades

7. Data-driven instructional decision making (Data Teams), including differentiating instruction for each level of language proficiency

What follows is an overview of each of the elements of a standards-based instruction and assessment model for English learners. Each element will be addressed in more detail in the chapters that follow.

**Content standards** currently exist for every core content area. The Common Core State Standards movement has helped to establish common achievement targets in the states that have adopted them. NCLB legislation has also required each state to develop a set of **English Language Proficiency Standards**. These standards set forth a progression from Beginning proficiency to Fluent or Advanced proficiency in English. While half of the states have developed their own standards, currently 25 states have become part of the WIDA (World-Class Instructional Design and Assessment) Consortium and share a set of language proficiency standards and language proficiency assessments.

**Priority Standards, or Power Standards,** as they were formerly termed, represent a subset of the entire list of content standards. They are prioritized standards that represent the nonnegotiable body of knowledge that students at a particular grade level need to master in order to be successful academically. The criteria we use to identify these priorities involve more than merely focusing our teaching on what students will be tested on on state achievement measures. In fact, it has been this myopic focus that has led classroom teachers down a frustratingly fruitless path of attempting to "cover" as much of the textbook as possible. Prioritizing the standards offers us an alternative—designing a curriculum that has at its core a set of prioritized and supporting standards that allow us to teach content to the depth and breadth that we know our students require and deserve. The process for prioritizing standards has us consider three criteria: school, life, and test. These criteria help us ensure the development of a balanced and rigorous curriculum. The first criterion, school, asks us to consider which standards represent essential prerequisite knowledge that our students will require in the following grade level or content area. Next, we consider which standards help build skills that are important in life, such as problem solving, reasoning, or critical thinking. Finally, we cross-reference our list with what we know students will be tested on and make any final additions. Our list of prioritized standards should represent about a third of the total number of standards for that content area. The prioritized standards will be taught deeply, while the others will be taught as supporting standards. In developing units of study, ESL teachers should identify prioritized **Language Proficiency Standards** that match the units of study they have identified. In this way, they will ensure that they have both language and content objectives for each unit of instruction.

**"Unwrapping" the content and language proficiency standards** refers to a process by which the concepts (nouns) and skills (verbs) that all students should know and be able to do are identified for a unit of instruction and its corresponding assessment. Content or self-contained mainstream teachers will focus on "unwrapping" the prioritized content standards, while ESL teachers will "unwrap" the pertinent language proficiency standards that align with their units of instruction. The Big Ideas and Essential Questions that come directly from the "unwrapped" content and language proficiency standards help focus and align instruction and assessment.

**Differentiated Common Formative Assessments** represent an assessment model in which teachers collaboratively design and administer assessments that are appropriate to the language proficiency level of ELLs. The process begins by creating one assessment, then differentiating that one assessment for the different levels of language proficiency. In this way, all students are working on the same assessment, only at their particular proficiency level. These formative assessments are administered while the learning is taking place. The results of these formative measures provide accurate, timely, and specific feedback to teachers and students that can be used to promote greater learning.

**Classroom Summative Assessments** provide the final confirmation that learning has taken place. These assessments are administered at the end of the instructional unit. The alignment between the common formative assessments and classroom summative assessments guarantees that they have predictive value in how students are going to perform on district and state summative assessment measures.

Finally, after creating the assessments, we are now ready to develop our **instructional unit of study**. The development of the instructional unit of study takes place after the "unwrapping" of the standards and after the creation of the assessments. In this way, we can ensure perfect alignment between standards, assessment, and instruction. In creating the instructional unit, teachers may develop differentiated performance assessments with accompanying scoring guides that help students show that they can apply the learning that has taken place during the course of the unit. The performance assessments also provide students with the feedback they need to reach proficiency.

After the administration of the common formative pre- or post-assessments, teachers meet to **collaboratively score student work** and analyze the results of the assessments in order to determine the next steps in the instructional sequence. Collaborative scoring of constructed-response items, in particular, helps teachers develop a common understanding of proficiency. For English learners, the issue of **differentiated grading** should be explored. If the true purpose of grades is to communicate progress, then wouldn't a differentiated grade by language proficiency level provide more accurate feedback to parents and students than an endless string of nonproficient grades? The issue of equitable grading practices for English learners will be more closely examined in Chapter 8.

**Data-driven instructional decision making** takes place after the administration of the common formative assessment and involves the five-step Data Teams process (with an additional sixth step for monitoring) in order to help teachers use the data formatively. The **Data Teams process** includes the following steps:

**Step 1.** Collect and chart data. For ELLs, data should be organized by language proficiency level, as well as the traditional groupings that include Proficient, Close, Far to Go, and Intensive Support.

**Step 2.** Analyze the strengths and obstacles for each group.

**Step 3.** Set S.M.A.R.T. goals that are attainable for each group.

**Step 4.** Identify the research-based strategies for each group that will help students attain the goals we've established.

**Step 5.** Determine the results indicators that will serve to help us identify whether the strategies we've implemented are having the desired impact on student achievement.

**Step 6.** Set meeting dates to monitor and ensure that everyone is on target to reach their goals by the prescribed date.

## THE BIG PICTURE—
## DIFFERENT APPROACHES, ONE GOAL

Taking into account the Five Doors as well as the components that make up the Standards-Assessment Alignment Diagram, school leaders and teachers must decide where to begin the process. The circle diagram in Exhibit 2.3, How Powerful Practices Work Together for English Language Learners, takes all of the elements outlined above and shows how they work together to form the basis of an aligned assessment and instruction system.

Deciding where to begin the process should entail evaluating what makes most sense for the needs of the students and staff. It should also include reflecting about the current state of the school system and what the logical first step should be based upon that evaluation. Three possible starting points are shared in the following paragraphs.

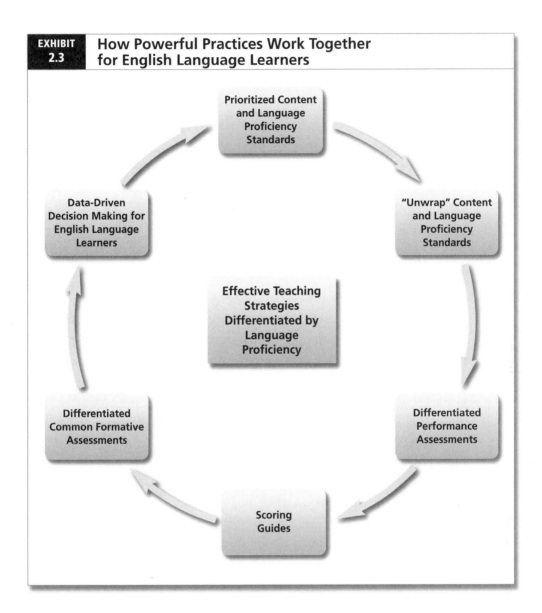

| EXHIBIT 2.3 | How Powerful Practices Work Together for English Language Learners |

## Clearly Articulated Achievement Standards—Begin with Prioritized Content and Language Proficiency Standards

In this approach, school systems use their professional judgment guided by the three criteria of endurance, leverage, and readiness to identify the content standards that are the highest priority for each grade level and content area. State assessment data is reviewed and helps to determine whether any modifications need to be made. Finally, for ESL teachers, the language proficiency standards are aligned with units of instruction, and the content and language proficiency standards are "unwrapped" together. Content and self-contained mainstream teachers can use the Assessment Matrices in

Chapter 7 to help them differentiate their common formative assessments after they've followed this process for their content area. The sequence is as follows:

1. Identify the content and language proficiency standards that represent the highest priorities based upon the criteria of endurance (life), leverage (test), and readiness (school).

2. Analyze state assessment data, including AMAO data, for English learners to determine the standards on which English learners may be scoring low or standards that may be weighted more heavily than others.

3. Modify the final list of content and language proficiency standards based upon the analysis of state assessment and AMAO data.

4. "Unwrap" the prioritized content standards along with the language proficiency standards. Determine the Big Ideas and Essential Questions that will help to guide and focus instruction and assessment.

5. Identify differentiated, research-based effective teaching strategies that will help students master the "unwrapped" concepts and skills as well as the Big Ideas.

6. ESL teachers develop common formative assessments that fully assess the "unwrapped" concepts and skills of the prioritized content and language proficiency standards. Content and self-contained mainstream teachers use the Assessment Matrices in Chapter 7 to help develop differentiated assessment tasks aligned to their common formative assessments, particularly for ELLs at Level 1, Pre-Production, and Level 2, Early Production.

7. Administer common formative assessments to determine student understanding of "unwrapped" concepts, skills, and language objectives while the learning is taking place. Provide timely, accurate, and specific feedback to students regarding their progress.

8. Analyze the results of common formative assessments using the five-step Data Teams process. Repeat the process.

## Clearly Articulated Achievement Standards—Begin with "Unwrapping" the Content and Language Proficiency Standards

In this second approach, teams of teachers begin by "unwrapping" all content and language proficiency standards. This enables educators to closely analyze the content of each standard in order to best identify the priorities. In a perfect world, where time was of no consequence, every team of teachers would be provided with the time to be able to "unwrap" all content and language proficiency standards before prioritizing. After "unwrapping," the standards are prioritized and then they are cross-referenced with state assessment and AMAO data. The steps in the sequence are as follows:

1. ESL teachers begin by "unwrapping" all content-area and language proficiency standards in order to identify the concepts and skills that students should know and be able to do. Content and self-contained mainstream teachers "unwrap" all content-area standards. Determine the Big Ideas and Essential Questions that will help guide and focus instruction and assessment.

2. Determine the concepts and skills from the content and language proficiency standards that are nonnegotiable for each grade level or content area. Identify the standards containing those concepts and skills and make those your priority standards.

3. Continue around the circle diagram from this point.

4. Analyze state assessment and AMAO data to find areas in which students have scored low, and identify the standards that receive the highest emphasis.

5. Cross-reference any of the areas of need on the state test with the list of identified priority standards and make revisions accordingly.

## Accurate Information about Student Achievement—Begin with Data

The third approach involves beginning the process with an analysis of state content and AMAO data. Since Adequate Yearly Progress is determined by a school's performance on state standardized measures, and AMAOs play an important part of this process, this approach makes most sense to some schools. The first three steps in the sequence are as follows:

1. Analyze state assessment data, including AMAO data, to determine areas in which students have scored low. It is best to analyze data over a two- to three-year period to see if any trends exist that may point to areas of need.

2. Identify the content and language proficiency standards that represent the areas of need identified by the state assessment data. These standards are the priority standards for that grade or content area.

3. ESL teachers "unwrap" the prioritized content and language proficiency standards to identify the concepts and skills that students will need to master, and determine the Big Ideas and Essential Questions that will help to guide and focus instruction. Content and self-contained mainstream teachers "unwrap" the prioritized content standards and determine the Big Ideas and Essential Questions that guide and focus instruction.

It is important for educators to consider that if the priority standards they've identified are only those that students will be tested on, then the standards that have been left out may be those that are important to success in school, as well as those that are life skills. A well-balanced list of priority standards should reflect not only what students will be tested on, but should also take into account skills that are important for success in school and skills that help students to succeed in life.

## THE STANDARDS-ASSESSMENT ALIGNMENT DIAGRAM— WHAT'S DIFFERENT FOR ENGLISH LEARNERS?

The Standards-Assessment Alignment Diagram proposed by Larry Ainsworth and Daniel Viegut in *Common Formative Assessments: How to Connect Standards-Based Instruction and Assessment* (2006) clearly illustrates an aligned system beginning with the state standards and ending with the state assessment. Only slight differences exist in the Standards-Assessment Alignment Diagram for English learners; however, they are significant enough that teachers should be aware of those differences. We will first examine the differences in the diagram for ESL teachers. For example, in addition to beginning with the state standards, when designing aligned instruction and assessment opportunities for ELLs, ESL teachers must also begin with the state's language proficiency standards. This serves two purposes: first, it ensures that every unit of instruction, and thus every lesson, contains language objectives as well as content knowledge objectives; second, it also ensures that the common formative assessments are aligned with summative assessments, as well as benchmarks and state tests, thus ensuring that our assessments will provide predictive value as to how English learners will perform on measures of state language proficiency.

The sequenced steps that appear in Exhibit 2.4 are described in greater detail following the exhibit. These steps will also be addressed in detail in the chapters that follow.

1. ESL teachers begin with state content and language proficiency standards. Use the criteria of school, life, and state test to prioritize.

2. Identify a list of priority content standards as well as priority language proficiency standards. These standards form the foundation for an aligned standards and assessment system.

3. "Unwrap" the priority content standards along with the priority language proficiency standards. This helps establish content and language objectives for each lesson within an instructional unit of study.

4. Work collaboratively within a Data Team to design a common formative pre- and post-assessment based on the priority content standards. Use the

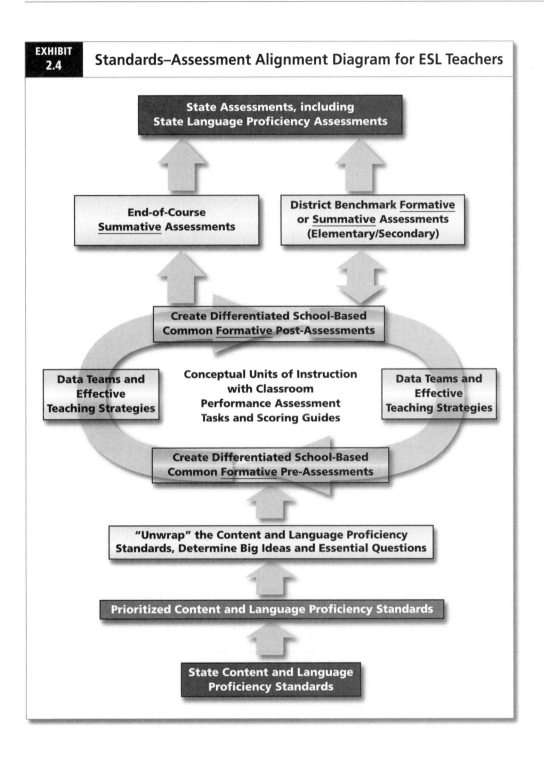

**EXHIBIT 2.4**

## Standards–Assessment Alignment Diagram for ESL Teachers

State Assessments, including State Language Proficiency Assessments

End-of-Course Summative Assessments

District Benchmark Formative or Summative Assessments (Elementary/Secondary)

Create Differentiated School-Based Common Formative Post-Assessments

Data Teams and Effective Teaching Strategies

Conceptual Units of Instruction with Classroom Performance Assessment Tasks and Scoring Guides

Data Teams and Effective Teaching Strategies

Create Differentiated School-Based Common Formative Pre-Assessments

"Unwrap" the Content and Language Proficiency Standards, Determine Big Ideas and Essential Questions

Prioritized Content and Language Proficiency Standards

State Content and Language Proficiency Standards

prioritized language proficiency standards to differentiate the common formative assessment for all levels of language proficiency. In this way, educators create one assessment, then differentiate it for the five levels of language acquisition. This makes more instructional sense than trying to create six different assessments per instructional unit.

5. Administer the common formative pre-assessment and analyze pre-assessment data in Data Teams. Analyze strengths and obstacles for each level of language proficiency. Write S.M.A.R.T. goals and identify strategies for each level of language proficiency that will help students meet the established goals.

6. Design conceptual units of instruction and include language objectives from the prioritized and "unwrapped" language proficiency standards. Design performance-based assessment opportunities with tasks written for each level of language proficiency along with accompanying scoring guides.

7. Teach the conceptual units of instruction and conduct formative assessment checks along the way.

8. Administer the differentiated common formative post-assessments.

9. Analyze post-assessment data in Data Teams. Compare pre- and post-assessment data and determine whether each language proficiency group met its goals. Identify the strategies to replicate. Reflect on the process and make plans for further improvements.

10. Repeat Steps 3 through 9 for the next instructional unit.

11. Deliberately align common formative assessments with district benchmark assessments and/or end-of-course assessments. This step may happen earlier in the design process. Again, if this measure is to be used formatively, then some effort should be made to differentiate the district benchmark assessment for English learners, especially for Levels 1 and 2 where students possess limited language skills.

12. Administer district benchmark assessments; analyze the results in Data Teams. If the results are used formatively, then they can be used to inform instruction.

13. Use state assessment blueprints, current and prior-year state test data, and released state assessment items to align benchmark and end-of-course assessments with the annual state assessments. This alignment typically takes place earlier in the year in order to ensure a deliberate alignment among classroom, district, and state assessments.

# THE STANDARDS-ASSESSMENT ALIGNMENT DIAGRAM FOR CONTENT AND SELF-CONTAINED TEACHERS OF ENGLISH LEARNERS

Exhibit 2.5 shows the same process as it would be carried out by those teachers who are content-area or self-contained mainstream teachers of English learners. In this case, these teachers have English learners sitting in their classrooms but may not be familiar or comfortable with creating differentiated assessments by level of language proficiency. We will assume that the teachers are using the language proficiency standards as well as sheltered instructional strategies to make the content comprehensible to their English learners; however, assessment becomes a particular challenge when students, especially at the beginning levels of language proficiency, have limited language skills with which to successfully complete a common formative assessment. In this case, the teacher follows the process as it appears in the original Standards-Assessment Alignment Diagram (see Exhibit 2.2). Once she has developed a common formative pre- and post-assessment, she can use the Assessment Matrices in Chapter 7 to help differentiate her assessment for students at different language proficiency levels. In essence, the assessment will remain unchanged for English learners at Levels 4 and 5 since they are approaching proficiency in English, but will be differentiated for Levels 1 through 3. This will ensure that all students receive the critical feedback provided by formative assessment that will help propel their content knowledge forward. Let's look more closely at each step shown in Exhibit 2.5.

1. Content and self-contained mainstream teachers begin with state content standards. Use the criteria of school, life, and state test to prioritize.

2. Identify a list of priority content standards. These standards form the foundation for an aligned instruction and assessment system for all students.

3. "Unwrap" the priority content standards. This helps establish content objectives for each lesson within an instructional unit of study.

4. Work collaboratively within a Data Team to design a common formative pre- and post-assessment based on the priority content standards. Use the Assessment Matrices in Chapter 7 to differentiate the common formative assessment for English learners, particularly at Levels 1 through 3 where language skills are most limited. In this way, educators create one assessment, then differentiate it for the applicable levels of acquisition. This makes more instructional sense than trying to create different assessments for different levels of English acquisition.

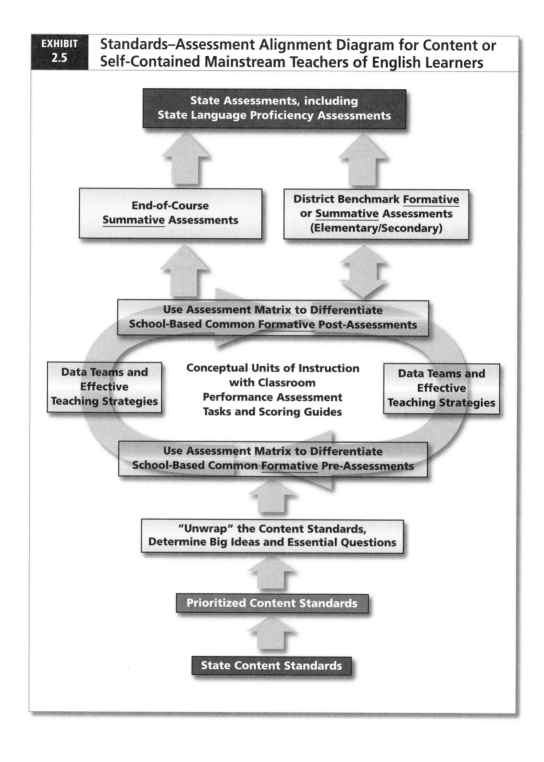

**EXHIBIT 2.5** Standards–Assessment Alignment Diagram for Content or Self-Contained Mainstream Teachers of English Learners

State Assessments, including State Language Proficiency Assessments

End-of-Course Summative Assessments

District Benchmark Formative or Summative Assessments (Elementary/Secondary)

Use Assessment Matrix to Differentiate School-Based Common Formative Post-Assessments

Data Teams and Effective Teaching Strategies

Conceptual Units of Instruction with Classroom Performance Assessment Tasks and Scoring Guides

Data Teams and Effective Teaching Strategies

Use Assessment Matrix to Differentiate School-Based Common Formative Pre-Assessments

"Unwrap" the Content Standards, Determine Big Ideas and Essential Questions

Prioritized Content Standards

State Content Standards

5. Administer the common formative pre-assessment and analyze pre-assessment data in Data Teams. Analyze strengths and obstacles for each applicable level of language proficiency. Write S.M.A.R.T. goals and identify strategies for each level of language proficiency that will help students meet the established goals.

6. Design conceptual units of instruction from the prioritized and "unwrapped" content standards. Use sheltered instructional strategies to ensure that the content is comprehensible to students at all language acquisition levels. Design performance-based assessment opportunities with tasks written for students at Levels 1 through 3 of language proficiency along with accompanying scoring guides.

7. Teach the conceptual units of instruction and conduct formative assessment checks along the way.

8. Administer the differentiated common formative post-assessments.

9. Analyze post-assessment data in Data Teams. Compare pre- and post-assessment data and determine whether all students met their goals. Identify the strategies to replicate. Reflect on the process and make plans for further improvements.

10. Repeat Steps 3 through 9 for the next instructional unit.

11. Deliberately align common formative assessments with district benchmark assessments and/or end-of-course assessments. This step may happen earlier in the design process. Again, if this measure is to be used formatively, then some effort should be made to differentiate the district benchmark assessment for English learners, especially for Levels 1 through 3 where students possess limited language skills.

12. Administer district benchmark assessments; analyze the results in Data Teams. If the results are used formatively, then they can be used to inform instruction.

13. Use state assessment blueprints, current and prior-year state test data, and released state assessment items to align benchmark and end-of-course assessments with the annual state assessments. This alignment typically takes place earlier in the year in order to ensure a deliberate alignment among classroom, district, and state assessments.

# CONCLUSION

Ultimately, our goal in differentiating our common formative assessments is to help English learners at all levels demonstrate understanding and mastery of content-area objectives. By providing differentiated learning and assessment opportunities we help our English learners not only advance their content knowledge but also their language proficiency in each of the four domains: Listening, Speaking, Reading, and Writing. In the following chapter we will examine the current state of assessment for English learners and what implications it has for their achievement. We will also explore the urgent need for differentiated formative assessments.

# DISCUSSION QUESTIONS

1. Whether using the Five Doors to an Aligned Assessment System (Exhibit 2.1) or the Standards-Assessment Alignment Diagram (Exhibit 2.2), have we determined where we are in the process of implementing a well-aligned and balanced assessment system? Have we determined where we are in implementing that same system for English learners?

2. Given the different approaches to starting the process, which one makes most sense for our school or district? Will we begin with prioritized content and language proficiency standards? Or with "unwrapping" the content and language proficiency standards? Or will we begin with the data?

3. Is there a common understanding at our school or district that the English learners at our site belong to ALL teachers and not just the ESL teacher? If not, why not? What are the major obstacles to coming to this understanding, and what are some first steps we can take as a staff?

4. Have ESL teachers been provided with the time and resources needed to use the Standards-Assessment Alignment Diagram to help them design aligned and appropriately differentiated common formative assessments that will help them monitor student progress toward language proficiency?

5. Have content-area or self-contained mainstream teachers been provided with the time and resources needed to use the Assessment Matrices to help them develop differentiated common formative assessments for English learners at Levels 1 through 3?

# CHAPTER 3
# Assessment Literacy

Prior to the development of a common formative assessment, it is imperative that we all possess a common level of assessment literacy. As mentioned previously, amid the deluge of instructional initiatives there exist as many definitions of those initiatives as there are teachers on a given campus. For that reason, we begin by establishing some common knowledge about assessment so that at our school site or within our grade-level team we can all share a common definition of what we mean by the term *common formative assessment*.

Assessment is an integral part of the instructional process. It provides critical feedback to the learner as well as to the teacher. In John Hattie's book *Visible Learning* (2009), a synthesis of over 800 meta-analyses on educational strategies, he states that feedback on student performance has an effect size of .73 and formative assessment has an effect size of .90 (p. 7). So how does effect size translate into increased learning and achievement in the classroom? Hattie has perhaps one of the clearest explanations: "An effect size of $d = 1.0$ indicates an increase of one standard deviation. . . . A one standard deviation increase is typically associated with advancing children's achievement by two to three years" (p. 7). Hattie continues, "An effect size of 1.0 would mean that, on average, students receiving the treatment would exceed 84 percent of students not receiving the treatment" (p. 8). These are unquestionably high-impact strategies that when implemented well can make a tremendous difference for all students, but in particular for English learners.

## ASSESSMENT TYPES

There are two major forms of assessment, formative and summative. Stiggins et al. (2005) distinguish the two by referring to formative assessment as "assessment *for* learning" and summative assessment as "assessment *of* learning." While they clearly state that both are essential components of the instructional process, they are proponents of a balanced assessment system. The question we should be asking ourselves is, "Do we currently have a balanced assessment system in our classrooms?" Upon closer examination of the two types of assessments, most of us will find that we currently do a great deal of summative assessment and not as much formative assessment. The best type of assessment to use depends on the answers to three basic questions: *Why assess? Assess what?* and *Assess how?* (See Exhibit 3.1).

The type of assessment is determined not only by the purpose of the assessment but also by the uses of the results. Summative assessment takes place at the conclusion of teaching to determine whether students have mastered a standard. The results of summative assessments are typically used for accountability purposes, such as determining grades. By contrast, formative assessment takes place while the learning is happening. The results of formative assessments are not used for accountability purposes and are therefore ungraded. Instead, the results of formative assessments are used to diagnose student needs, plan next steps in the instructional process, and provide students with detailed feedback they can use to propel their learning forward. The results of formative assessments help both teachers and students make those invaluable midcourse corrections that are necessary to ensure that learning takes place. By contrast, the results of summative assessments cannot help students or teachers change course since by nature the results come too late in the learning process to make a difference.

Similarly, James Popham (2008) defines formative assessment as a planned process in which assessment-elicited evidence of student learning is used by teachers to adjust their ongoing instructional processes and by students to adjust their

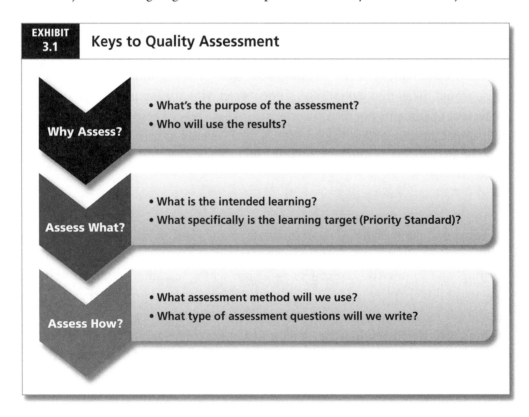

**EXHIBIT 3.1    Keys to Quality Assessment**

**Why Assess?**
- What's the purpose of the assessment?
- Who will use the results?

**Assess What?**
- What is the intended learning?
- What specifically is the learning target (Priority Standard)?

**Assess How?**
- What assessment method will we use?
- What type of assessment questions will we write?

current learning tactics (p. 6). He goes on to stress the fact that formative assessment is a process, not an event. Within this process, the learner is provided with valuable information as to how he can close the gap between where he currently is in the learning process and where he needs to be (p. 6). The implication here is that, again, like Stiggins et al., the distinguishing factor between formative and summative assessment is that in the case of formative assessment both teachers and students use the feedback provided by the assessment to improve upon the learning taking place.

## WHAT ARE COMMON FORMATIVE ASSESSMENTS?

Common formative assessments are formative assessments that are collaboratively designed by grade-level teams or departments. Teachers work together to decide upon the learning targets, then take those learning targets and design formative assessments that can be administered along the way during the learning process. They are short-cycle assessments of no more than two priority standards containing between three and five items per standard, depending on the complexity of the standard(s), and are often developed in a pre- or post-test design model. The results are then analyzed collaboratively and provide valuable information to teachers as to any adjustments that may need to be made in the teaching of the content. I am often asked to show teachers an example of a common formative assessment, and I explain that what distinguishes a common formative assessment from a summative assessment is not the assessment itself, but rather how the results are used. If the results are used to enter a grade into a grade book, pass back to the students, then continue with the next topic of study the very next day, then the assessment is a summative assessment. If, instead, the assessment is scored and the results are used collaboratively by a team of teachers to decide upon next steps in the learning plan, and if the results are shared with students so that they receive diagnostic feedback about the gap between where they are in the learning process as compared to where they need to be and the steps needed to close that gap, then the assessment is a common formative assessment.

## WHAT COMMON FORMATIVE ASSESSMENT IS NOT

For clarity's sake, let's also be sure that we understand what common formative assessment is not. Popham (2008) says that it is not a series of interim assessments administered to all students periodically by a school or district and often mislabeled as formative assessments (p. 6). He continues by adding that formative assessment is also not what takes place when a teacher makes an instructional adjustment based on a sense that students are confused. In other words, formative assessment is more than a "gut feeling" based upon a classroom full of puzzled faces staring back at you. While every good teacher uses those signals as a way to adjust his teaching in the moment, common formative assessment takes deliberate thought and planning.

It is also important to note that a common formative assessment is more than just an "assessment in common." While it is certain that if two teachers are teaching out of the same textbook they will most likely be using the same assessments, this is not what is implied by common formative assessments. Common formative assessments are part of a well-thought-out assessment process that is student centered. This means that teachers have worked together to analyze the learning targets, or priority standards, and have "unwrapped" the standards into skills and concepts along with levels of Bloom's Taxonomy. In doing this work, teachers get at the heart of what they need to teach and begin to develop a common definition of proficiency. Now, while it may make sense to begin by looking at the assessments that are part of the textbook, it is also critical that teachers ask some tough questions about the alignment of those assessments. Questions such as:

- How many items are on the assessment? Of those items, how many are directly aligned to the priority standard(s)?
- Are all parts of the priority standard addressed on this assessment?
- Do the questions assess the standard at the appropriate level of cognition (Bloom's Taxonomy)?
- Is the priority standard assessed in a variety of ways—that is, selected response, constructed response?
- Will the assessment provide sufficient and appropriate feedback to the student? Teacher?

Once these questions have been answered, teachers can decide whether to use the existing assessment as is, as a starting point, or whether they may need to create a new assessment altogether. Clearly, this process involves more than merely having and using an assessment in common.

## COMMON SUMMATIVE ASSESSMENTS

Although there is little written about common summative assessments (CSAs), I do encourage teams of teachers to develop them as well as common formative assessments. These common summative assessments can be used for grading purposes as well as for informing teachers, students, and parents about how well students are doing in a particular content area. In addition, the information gleaned from these collaboratively designed assessments can be used to improve student learning and teacher practice, and to help decide about the effectiveness of curricular materials and programs. As opposed to common formative assessments, CSAs cover a longer period of study and more standards and are administered at the conclusion of the learning process. Although the common formative assessment assesses only the priority standards, the CSA may assess both priority and supporting standards. Again, teams of teachers should begin with existing chapter or unit assessments from their textbook series. As is the case when using textbook assessments for formative assessment, questions should be asked regarding the items on the assessment:

- Are all the standards that were taught within this unit of study sufficiently represented on the assessment?

- Do the items align to the standards?

- Are the standards assessed in multiple ways? Is there a nice balance between selected- and constructed-response items?

## CHOOSING THE RIGHT ASSESSMENT FOR THE PURPOSE

We know what our purpose is and we've identified and "unwrapped" the learning targets/priority standards. Now it's time to decide why we're assessing and determine whether our assessment will be summative or formative. Once we know our purpose (Assess why?) and have identified the targets (Assess what?), then we are ready to begin designing the assessment (Assess how?).

In their book *Common Formative Assessments*, Ainsworth and Viegut (2006) identify and define some of the major types of assessment used regularly in K–12 schools.

- **Large-scale (external) assessments** are developed outside of the local school or district. They are summative assessments administered annually, typically for accountability purposes. The results of these assessments are usually not received for months after their administration.

- **Small-scale (internal) assessments** are developed within a school or district and are designed to provide a snapshot of student learning of standards as of a particular point in time. Typically referred to as benchmark assessments, the timing of their administration and how the results are used determine whether these assessments are formative or summative.

- **Norm-referenced assessments** are referred to as standardized tests. Rather than comparing student performance to an objective standard, they compare student performance to a larger "norm group" of students representing a diverse national cross section. These summative assessments are used to rank-order students, schools, and districts in relation to the "norm group."

- **Criterion-referenced assessments** are state or district tests that are aligned to state and/or district standards. They are used to determine how well individual students and groups of students have mastered a specific set of learning targets. The results of these assessments are used to rank students according to set levels of performance. (pp. 56–57)

Within any type of assessment, test developers can choose to use different methods to assess the learning targets. The method selected should be reflective of the type of learning target. Stiggins et al. tell us that if, for example, a teacher is assessing a learning target at the lowest level of Bloom's Taxonomy, where the student is being asked to merely recall information, then it would not be very appropriate or wise to assess that standard using a performance assessment, because a performance assessment is so involved (p.100). Let's take a closer look at the different types of assessment items.

- **Selected-response** items require students to select an answer from a provided list. While multiple choice is the most common form of selected response, it is important to remember the other types of selected-response items, including true-false, matching, or fill-in (from a provided list of options). Selected response is the best option for assessing knowledge targets, main concepts, and basic skills, as well as for higher-level targets such as when assessing understanding of patterns of reasoning. If the learning target involves the performance of a skill (e.g., reading a passage fluently) or the ability to create a product (e.g., writing a narrative), then selected-response items would not be appropriate (unless the focus was on the prerequisite skills involved in the task) (Stiggins, et. al., 2005, p. 100). Overdependence on selected-response items tends to promote memorization of factual information rather than higher-level thinking skills (Popham, 2003).

- **Constructed-response** items require students to use knowledge and skills to answer a question or complete a task. Students are asked to construct a response in either of the following formats: short answer, open response, extended written response, or fill-in (with **no** provided list of options). Constructed-response items are more likely to show whether or not students can apply what they are learning (Ainsworth and Viegut, 2006, p. 57), and will typically require the development and use of a scoring guide. Student responses often provide a window into students' reasoning, which helps teachers uncover misconceptions (Stiggins, et. al., 2005, p. 100). Constructed-response items will require more time to create, administer, and score.

- **Performance assessment** items require students to use critical thinking skills to construct a response, create a product, or perform a task as a way of demonstrating proficiency. These assessment items require the use of a scoring guide, provided to students in advance of completing the task, to determine proficiency. Because the tasks within a performance assessment apply content knowledge and skills to real-world situations, they can be highly engaging and motivational for students. The best performance assessment items offer multiple opportunities for students to revise their work using the feedback provided by peer- and self-assessment opportunities (Ainsworth and Viegut, 2006).

## APPLYING ASSESSMENT LITERACY TO THE CREATION OF A COMMON FORMATIVE ASSESSMENT

Armed with assessment literacy, we are now ready to examine the process of creating a common formative assessment from beginning to end. Remember that the first order of business is deciding what type of assessment is most appropriate for our purpose (Assess why?). The next twelve steps delineate the planning steps teachers should follow when designing a standards-based conceptual unit. Considerations for planning instruction and assessment for English learners have been embedded within this twelve-step design process.

1. Identify the priority standard being taught in the upcoming unit of study.

2. Identify other related standards—even ESL teachers should consider interdisciplinary standards to drive the unit of study. In this way, language is taught within the context of meaningful content, and not in isolation. Hill and Flynn (2006) remind us that it is critical to set both content and language objectives for ELLs. Because ELLs are learning content while they learn the English language, it is important for ESL teachers to remember that just as language learning cannot occur if we only focus on content, content knowledge cannot grow if we only focus on learning the English language (p. 22).

3. "Unwrap" the standards to identify the specific concepts and skills included within the standards. Identify the level of rigor of the standards by identifying the level of Bloom's Taxonomy represented by each skill. ESL teachers

should "unwrap" the prioritized English Language Development standards along with any applicable interdisciplinary prioritized content standards that apply to the unit of instruction.

4. Determine the Big Ideas based on the "unwrapped" standards that represent what we want students to realize on their own by the end of the instructional unit.

5. Write the matching Essential Questions for each Big Idea. These questions help drive and focus instruction for teachers.

These initial five steps help teachers to answer the question, Assess what?, and help teachers identify the instructional focus for the unit of instruction. Our next seven steps, 6 through 12, will help us to design aligned units of instruction as well as decide the type of assessment that best answers the third and final question, *Assess how?*.

6. Review and evaluate the different types of assessment formats and item types. Giving special consideration to the type of assessment is especially important. For example, ESL teachers will want to take into account the use of the English Language Development standards specifically if they are assessing language proficiency. On the other hand, content-area or self-contained mainstream teachers can use the Assessment Matrices in Chapter 7 to help them differentiate an existing common formative assessment, particularly for Level 1, Pre-Production, and Level 2, Early Production, students. We will learn more about this in Chapter 4.

7. Select the assessment item types that will provide the most credible evidence that the student has mastered the "unwrapped" concepts and skills, or learning targets. The best assessments contain a mix of selected- and constructed-response items.

8. Collaboratively create the pre- and post-assessment items. Ensure that the assessment contains enough items to be able to infer whether a student is proficient or not. ESL teachers create differentiated assessment items based on language level. Content-area teachers and self-contained mainstream teachers use the Assessment Matrices to write differentiated pre- and post-assessment items/tasks, particularly for Level 1 and Level 2 students.

9. Administer the pre-assessment. Score and analyze the results collaboratively.

10. Using the pre-assessment results, plan daily lessons and learning activities that will get students to master the "unwrapped" concepts and skills. Content-area and self-contained mainstream teachers develop differentiated content lessons for ELLs that ensure that they can access the content.

11. Teach the unit, formatively assess during the course of the unit, and continue using differentiated instructional strategies to meet the needs of all students, including ELLs.

12. Administer the post-assessment. Score and analyze the results collaboratively. Plan intervention, remediation, or reteaching based upon the results and focused on the "unwrapped" priority standards.

The final and most important step in the process involves communicating the results of these common formative assessments. Teams of teachers must decide what information would be most valuable to students and what form that feedback should take.

## PUTTING THE PIECES TOGETHER—ALIGNMENT OF STANDARDS, INSTRUCTION, AND ASSESSMENT

The alignment of standards, instruction, and assessment is a vital component of this process that must be deliberately planned. As with so many other school initiatives, my question about alignment is often met with an exasperated, "Of course we have an aligned curriculum, instruction, and assessment system in place." Upon closer investigation, I often find that alignment is actually an illusion, as far from reality as PLCs often are. So what does it look like when we have true alignment, and how do we make it happen?

### Standards

First of all, as has been mentioned in previous chapters, we begin by defining a set of prioritized standards that represent the nonnegotiables for each grade level and in each content area. While this step makes sense, and most educators will agree with it, what we find in most schools is an incoherent curriculum where teachers are attempting to teach too many topics without any depth of understanding. This "mile-wide-inch-deep" curriculum has not served us well, as we shall see when we examine national assessment results in Chapter 4. If it seems to make so much sense, then what is keeping us from doing it? Mike Schmoker (2011) writes that it is neither lack of resources, nor the lack of time (p. 28). Instead, he cites Odden (2009) as saying that it is the lack of "will and persistence" to implement what we already know works (p. 22). Schmoker reminds us that we have 12 years with our students amounting to almost 1,000 instructional hours per year, but that unfortunately much of that time is squandered on nonacademic activities. He reminds us that a curriculum that prepares students for college, careers, and citizenship in the 21st century requires meaningful opportunities for reading, writing, speaking, and thinking, all focused on a coherent body of content in the subject areas (p. 28). While I am often approached by leery educators who wonder if by identifying priority standards we are somehow leaving something out that students may be tested on, I am quick to refer them to Doug Reeves' (2004) contention that a good set of priority standards addresses about 88 percent of what students will encounter on a state test, but not 100 percent. By attempting to go after that additional 12 percent, we will have too many standards to cover and will have less time for those standards that are most essential. This again forces us into covering too much content and not providing students with the opportunity to learn anything deeply. In contrast, a focus on the most essential standards promotes both deep learning and higher test scores.

Along with the prioritized standards, Schmoker cites research by David Conley, found in his book *College Knowledge* (2005), that points to four intellectual standards through which all others should be taught:

1. Read to infer/interpret/draw conclusions.

2. Support arguments with evidence.

3. Resolve conflicting views encountered in source documents.

4. Solve complex problems with no obvious answer.

If thoughtfully matched with content-area priority standards, these four standards could inform and drive the reading, writing, speaking, listening, and thinking that students do on a daily basis, resulting in students who are critical thinkers, writers, readers, and problem solvers—ready to confidently face the challenges of a 21st-century world.

Once we have identified the priorities, we then "unwrap" them to get at the essence of the standards and to help teachers define proficiency. In so doing, we are able to answer the three questions related to the Curriculum portion of Exhibit 3.2. While questions 1 and 2 are clearly answered through the prioritizing and "unwrapping" process, question 3 tends to be the most elusive of the three questions. Question 3 implies, as Schmoker does, that we may be teaching content that is both unnecessary and extraneous. This is a difficult pill to swallow as we like to believe that everything we teach is of critical importance, when upon closer examination we might find that some content is indeed unnecessary, especially if it is not part of the standards or priority standards we are required to teach.

| EXHIBIT 3.2 | Alignment of Standards, Instruction, and Assessment |
|---|---|

1. What are the concepts and skills we want all students to learn?
2. How do our materials align to the concepts and skills in our "unwrapped" standards?
3. What will we stop teaching?

**Standards**

**Student Achievement**

**Instruction**

**Assessment**

1. How will we sequence our instruction to ensure mastery?
2. What strategies will we use?
3. How are we implementing the strategies?

1. How do we know if students have learned?
2. How do we respond when students don't learn?
3. How do we differentiate for students who already know the material?

## Assessment

Once we have identified the learning targets, we begin designing our assessments. Teams of teachers create common formative pre- and post-assessments that will help them determine strengths and weaknesses of students, set achievement goals, and identify effective teaching strategies to help get students to proficiency. We will learn more about the five-step Data Teams process we use to analyze our assessment results in Chapter 8. The three questions listed in Exhibit 3.2 related to Assessment guide the creation of our assessments. Essentially, our formative and summative assessments should address all three of these questions.

## Instruction

The third component of an aligned system is instruction. Instruction defines how we teach the learning targets, or prioritized standards. Once we have our assessments created and know what it is we expect from students as evidence of proficiency, we are ready to plan the instructional strategies and sequence of instruction we will follow to help students reach mastery. This is also known as backward mapping, or beginning with the end in mind. The three guiding questions related to Instruction in Exhibit 3.2 help keep us focused on what matters most—instruction. High-quality teaching has been shown to make more of a difference in student achievement than we might think. In fact, Hattie writes that an effective teacher is the single most important factor in educating students (2009). In other words, what teachers *do* matters. There is now an abundance of evidence that teachers are "the most important school factor in how much children learn" (Colvin and Johnson, 2007, p. 36). And Schmoker reminds us that an impressive amount of research confirms this: "It is now a well-established fact that even three years of fairly ordinary but effective teaching can completely change the trajectory of low-achieving students—vaulting them from the lowest to the highest quartile" (Hattie, 2009; Bracey, 2004; Sanders and Horn, 1994). The challenge is then in defining what effective instruction looks like. Effective instruction is not something elusive that happens in the classrooms of those lucky few teachers who are "born with it"; rather, the research is clear on what good instruction looks like. Effective instruction begins with a clear learning objective, teaching in small steps, or "chunks," and modeling, which are then followed by multiple cycles of guided practice and checks for understanding (Schmoker, 2011).

1. **Clear learning objective**. Nothing clarifies what we are teaching like the "unwrapping" process does. Not only does it break the standard down to the level of concepts and skills, but it also defines the level of rigor at which the

learning target needs to be taught. Clear learning objectives emerge from this process and clearly define the learning for teachers and students.

2. **Chunking the learning.** Once we "unwrap" the standard, we then develop the learning progression that will lead our students to mastery. This learning progression defines the small steps, or "chunks," that represent individual lessons.

3. **Modeling the learning.** This step involves teachers walking students through the learning using strategies such as "think alouds" in which they demonstrate for students the exact thought process that accompanies a skill. For example, if reading with a purpose is the objective, teachers model the process but then also the thinking that happens when one thinks critically as one reads.

4. **Guided practice with the concept or skill accompanied by feedback.** As with all newly acquired knowledge, practice is essential to mastery. However, note that the guided practice should always be followed by targeted and specific feedback that helps propel the learner forward in his learning. Teachers should be actively engaged in this step of the process. This is not the point at which we should be sitting at our desks getting caught up on the myriad tasks we are asked to complete in the course of a given day or week; in fact, it is the point at which we are needed most critically by our students.

There is nothing novel or earth-shattering about the elements of effective instruction; however, we need to ensure that rather than be tied to an instructional sequence as outlined in a textbook, we use our professional judgment as teachers to determine the sequence and lesson format that makes the most instructional sense for the group of students sitting in front of us.

## CONCLUSION

As with any new initiative, our first order of business when implementing common formative assessments is ensuring that our entire team or department shares a common definition. Once we've come to a common definition, it is important for us to build assessment literacy together. The work of such assessment experts as Stiggins, Popham, and Ainsworth, as presented in this chapter, can help a team develop a deeper understanding of formative assessment, which will in turn help them take the first few steps toward designing a well-aligned common formative assessment that meets the needs of all students.

## DISCUSSION QUESTIONS

1. How is our team currently defining assessment? Do we have a common understanding of formative assessment?

2. Does our team currently use the three guiding questions—Assess why?, Assess what?, and Assess how?—to drive the development of our assessments?

3. How do we currently use the results of our assessments? If we use them mainly for assigning grades, can we agree that we have an unbalanced assessment system made up of mostly summative assessments? Do we agree that we need to balance our assessments?

4. If our assessment system is unbalanced, how can we begin to use the results differently so that we can ensure that we have a more balanced assessment system?

5. What implications does the twelve-step design process have for teaching and learning for all students? English language learners?

6. Do we have an aligned curriculum, instruction, and assessment system? What evidence do we have that this is so? If not, what is a first step we will take toward making this a reality?

# CHAPTER 4

# Assessment and the English Language Learner

The No Child Left Behind Act of 2001 (NCLB) requires that all students, including English learners, reach proficiency in English language arts and math by 2014. Schools must ensure that English learners make continuous progress toward that goal annually or risk serious consequences. If English learners represent a large enough subgroup, then they are required to meet the growth targets set forth each year by the NCLB legislation for all subgroups. Additionally, English learners must meet AMAO growth targets annually (see Chapter 1). This covers the large-scale external, state standardized testing of English learners, but what about small-scale internal, site-based assessment for English learners? Before we can even begin to tackle the question of site-based assessment for ELLs, it is important that we understand the English learner status from the moment of identification all the way to reclassification out of the English learner subgroup.

Let's begin with the classification of a student as an English learner. In the last few years, some issues have been raised about the validity of Home Language Surveys (HLSs), the measure currently used as an initial screening tool, the first determinant of whether a child is potentially an English language learner. Professor Jamal Abedi of UCLA argues that because Home Language Surveys differ so much from state to state, and may in fact differ from district to district within a state, we struggle as a nation with the first order of business, which is defining and identifying English language learners (2008).

The current definition of an English language learner as set forth in the NCLB legislation is dependent upon two pieces of information: (1) the student's language background information and (2) his level of English proficiency. Information on the language background of students (for example, country of birth, native language, and type and frequency of any language other than English spoken at home) comes typically from a Home Language Survey that is completed by a parent. Home Language Surveys are developed by individual states and may differ slightly in wording from district to district. This lack of consistency prompts Dr. Abedi (2008) to raise concerns about the validity of the Home Language Survey (p. 18). If parents have had prior experiences enrolling their children in other states or districts, the inconsistency in language used on the Home Language Surveys could result in inaccurate responses with the potential consequence of the inaccurate placement of their child, which could have devastating effects on the child. This adds to the importance of ensuring clarity for parents regarding the completion of the Home Language Survey. Short and Fitzsimmons (2007) share these concerns and make some recommendations of their own. Because of the incredible diversity within a single school's population of English learners, they recommend revising the Home Language Survey to ensure that parents are providing more relevant information regarding their children, including:

- Native language skills

- Immigration generation

- Age of child at arrival in U.S. schools

- Mobility history that includes the number of times the student has left the country, how long the student was gone each time, whether the student attended school in his native country, and whether the student was enrolled back in U.S. schools between visits (p. 17)

This type of invaluable information when coupled with high-quality language proficiency assessments can help ensure the appropriate placement of ELLs.

Information about a student's level of English proficiency in listening, speaking, reading, writing, and comprehension comes from existing tests of English proficiency. However, as we have seen from the research, there are major concerns with the reliability and validity of these sources of information (Abedi, 2008). If so much controversy exists in the mere identification and definition of an English language learner, then the urgency for classroom teachers to have differentiated common formative assessments by level for their English learners is no longer an option but a necessity. How else are we to determine an ELL's proficiency accurately if so much doubt exists as to the validity of state and district identification systems? Common formative assessments used by ESL teachers, aligned to content and language proficiency standards, provide the timely, accurate, and specific feedback that ELLs require to be able to improve their performance and propel their acquisition of English to the next level. Common formative assessments of content knowledge, differentiated by content or self-contained classroom teachers, provide the necessary feedback to help English learners advance their knowledge in the content areas despite having limited English skills. Regardless of inconsistencies in initial identification or progress monitoring of language proficiency, we can create well-aligned assessments that accurately gauge the progress made by English learners either in acquiring English or in the content areas.

## WHAT ABOUT LARGE-SCALE
## EXTERNAL ASSESSMENTS?

As we read in Chapter 2, developing a well-aligned assessment system ensures that our assessments have predictive value and thus helps us anticipate how students will perform on large-scale external assessments. Unfortunately, for most districts across the country, this is not the case, particularly in regard to the alignment of assessments for English learners. Beginning this process is essential to changing the trajectory of learning for so many of our English learners, but especially for those who have entered high school ill-prepared and who are in danger of becoming drop-out statistics.

The U.S. Department of Education recently released its most current large-scale assessment results for the National Assessment of Educational Progress (NAEP), including 11-year trends, from 1998 to 2009. The results are nothing short of devastating.

Exhibit 4.1 shows the results in reading between 1998 and 2009 for ELL Hispanic students. As you can see, every subgroup has made some progress in those ten years; however, the achievement gap for Hispanic ELLs is persistent and begins to widen in eighth grade.

Exhibit 4.2 shows that the achievement gap is no better when we look at eighth-grade reading scores for native English speakers and English learners of all ethnicities, illustrating again the urgent need for implementation of high-impact strategies such as formative assessment and feedback in an effort to close the persistent gap.

This data confirms the findings of other researchers who have warned that rapid progress for ELLs in the early years brought on by submersing the students in English is not sustained when those same ELLs enter middle school. While submersion programs may result in ELLs being reclassified more quickly, the long-term prognosis for these students is not positive. As we see from the eighth-grade NAEP results, as the content becomes more complex, a large majority of this group of ELLs, many of whom may no longer be receiving ESL support, begin to struggle as a result of not having the academic language skills necessary for success in middle school and high school content classes. As mentioned in Chapter 1, many of these students end up becoming drop-out statistics. For those who choose to stay in school, oftentimes the support they need to be successful is difficult to come by. It is precisely these students who could greatly benefit from a well-aligned standards and assessment system that provides them the type of formative feedback they require to be successful.

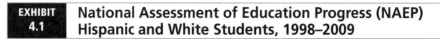

**EXHIBIT 4.1**

## National Assessment of Education Progress (NAEP) Hispanic and White Students, 1998–2009

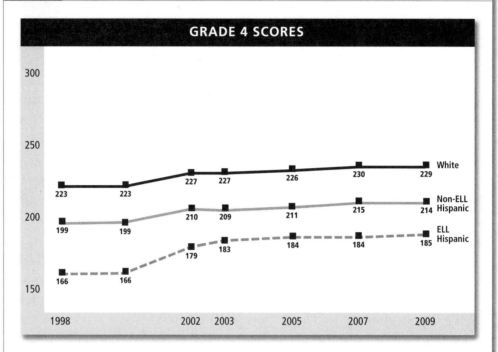

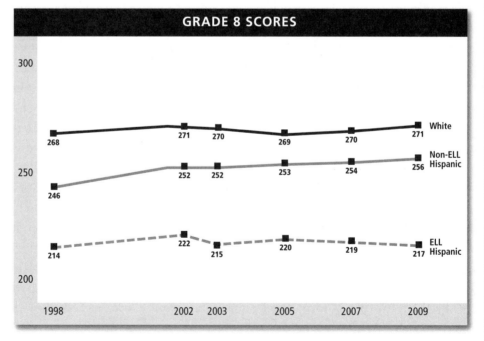

Source: U.S. Department of Education, 1998, 2002, 2003, 2005, 2007, 2009.

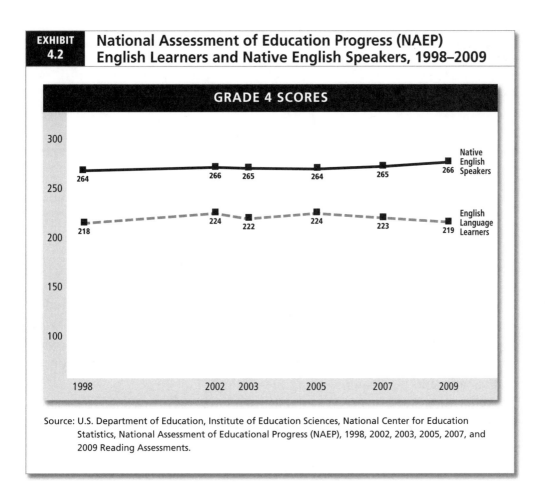

**EXHIBIT 4.2** National Assessment of Education Progress (NAEP) English Learners and Native English Speakers, 1998–2009

Source: U.S. Department of Education, Institute of Education Sciences, National Center for Education Statistics, National Assessment of Educational Progress (NAEP), 1998, 2002, 2003, 2005, 2007, and 2009 Reading Assessments.

## WHY ASSESS?

Currently, English learners in every state are assessed annually in the area of language acquisition. The state assessments are designed to provide districts with data on the English learner's progress in acquiring English; progress is assessed in each of the four domains of language: Listening, Speaking, Reading, and Writing, as well as comprehension (listening and reading). In addition to receiving scores in each of the domains, teachers also receive an overall score, which is typically the average of the scores in all four domains. For example, Exhibit 4.3 shows a typical score report for an English learner. Note the disparity in scores for this student, which is very common in the typical ELL profile. While Speaking and Listening characteristically receive the highest scores, in contrast the score for Writing is typically the lowest score because of the cognitive and language demands it involves. A teacher who has

| EXHIBIT 4.3 | Typical State Language Proficiency Assessment Results for Level 3 English Language Learners |
|---|---|

| Listening | Speaking | Reading | Writing | Overall Level |
|:---:|:---:|:---:|:---:|:---:|
| 3 | 4 | 3 | 2 | 3 |

this student in his content-area class may be puzzled by the fact that this student sounds great when conversing in class, however fails to complete reading and writing assignments. The teacher may infer that the student is lazy or withdrawn when in fact this student simply lacks the academic vocabulary needed to successfully complete assignments that require reading and writing.

While these assessments are certainly useful to some degree, like other large-scale external assessments, the results are often received months after the assessment was administered. Because language development is so fluid, it is likely that a student's language acquisition level may have changed in at least one domain between the time the assessment was administered and the time the results were received by the classroom teacher.

In most districts, the data received from the state language acquisition assessments are the only assessment data collected on an English learner in the course of a school year. After having established the effectiveness of feedback and formative assessment in Chapter 3 and presenting information on the persistent achievement gap between ELLs and native English speakers, we can see why both teachers and students could benefit greatly from the implementation of assessment strategies by both ESL and content teachers. In particular, it is critically important for ESL teachers to assess language proficiency periodically throughout the year in order to provide essential feedback to English learners as to their progress in acquiring English. Additionally, content teachers can provide critical feedback to English learners about their progress in learning content by differentiating classroom common formative assessments and providing targeted instruction at the students' appropriate language proficiency levels.

## THE CURRENT STATE OF ASSESSMENT FOR THE ENGLISH LANGUAGE LEARNER

First of all, it should be noted that according to research on best practices for English learners, assessing a student's content knowledge, particularly during the earliest levels of language acquisition, is best done in the student's primary language. Unfortunately, most teachers who work with English learners, particularly in content and self-contained mainstream classrooms, do not speak a second language, much less the 13 languages that may be represented by the ELLs in their classroom. This complicates the ability of teachers to create primary-language formative assessments, and most resort to having their Level 1 and Level 2 students skip the assessments altogether or encouraging them to give the assessments their "best shot." ESL teachers, on the other hand, are already dealing with increasing caseloads, which leaves them lacking the necessary time and resources to create differentiated language acquisition assessments that can be administered periodically throughout the year. They are instead left with one set of results on language acquisition that are typically outdated by the time they are received. Assessing language proficiency more than once a year is critically important if teachers expect to have accurate and timely data on which to base their instructional decisions. Likewise, content-area teachers should be able to assess all their students, including English learners, and provide detailed feedback to them as to their progress in learning the content. The design process introduced in Chapter 6 for ESL teachers and in Chapter 7 for content teachers will help both types of teachers effectively meet the assessment needs of their English learners.

## ASSESSMENT OF LANGUAGE PROFICIENCY VERSUS ASSESSMENT OF CONTENT KNOWLEDGE

Studies conducted by UCLA's National Center for Research on Evaluation, Standards and Student Testing (CRESST) have repeatedly shown that English language learners perform substantially lower on language arts tests compared to mathematics and science tests. Additionally, in controlled studies that measured the effects of accommodations, CRESST was able to repeatedly improve English learner performance by approximately 10 to 20 percent on many assessments. Modifying or simplifying the language of the test without reducing its rigor consistently resulted in English learner performance improvement (Abedi and Dietel, 2004, p. 4). These findings suggest to us that low English learner language proficiency decreases English learner performance on most tests, thus bringing into question the test as an accurate measure of English learner content knowledge. The assessment then becomes a measure of two skills for the English learner, content and language, and does not provide an accurate picture of the student's content mastery.

## IMPLICATIONS FOR THE ENGLISH LANGUAGE LEARNER

When differentiating common formative assessments, teachers of English learners must be sure to simplify the language of the assessment enough so that the students can comprehend the task or assignment. When scoring the assessment, teachers also need to be sure to score English learners on the content of their responses and not on their use of the English language. Assessment—the gathering and interpreting of information about students' knowledge, strengths, or obstacles in relation to a learning target or "unwrapped" priority standard—must be appropriate for the learners being assessed. Assessment systems must be designed with the whole English learner in mind, and must take into account the learner's language acquisition level so that an appropriate assessment task can be designed that truly assesses the student's content knowledge and not his use of the English language.

## THE URGENT NEED FOR DIFFERENTIATED FORMATIVE ASSESSMENTS

With differentiated common formative assessments, teachers use a variety of activities to check students' understanding, acknowledging that students learning a second language need a variety of ways to demonstrate their understanding of concepts that are not wholly reliant on advanced language skills. This allows the English learners, particularly at the earliest levels of language acquisition, to demonstrate what they know about the topic. More importantly, it allows teachers to provide feedback to English learners that helps them close the gap between where they are in the learning continuum and where they need to be. Additionally, the results of the assessment provide feedback to teachers as to the effectiveness of the instructional strategies they used to teach the content. If, for example, the teacher has been using sheltered instructional strategies, the results of the common formative assessment can provide valuable feedback to the teacher about the use of those strategies.

## CONCLUSION

From the moment English learners enter our schools, they are administered a series of assessments. These assessments are designed to help educators classify them and determine their level of language proficiency. Other than these mostly large-scale external language proficiency assessments, most schools have few resources to help provide small-scale internal assessments that could be used formatively to help advance the learning of students with limited proficiency in English. As a result, we see from recently released NAEP scores that English learners have made little progress and that, in fact, the achievement gap continues to persist between them and native English speakers. Research conducted by CRESST has shown that accommodations in language can help English learners more successfully complete assessment tasks, which in turn helps them get the formative feedback they require and deserve. The implications for classroom teachers from these studies are significant. They confirm what so many teachers have suspected for so long—that asking English learners to take an assessment for which they lack the language skills is at best a waste of time, and at worst potentially harmful if it diminishes the students' motivation to learn. The answer, then, is for classroom teachers to be given a process for differentiating existing common formative assessments that does not require an unreasonable investment of time, and that allows English learners to grow academically and, once and for all, close the achievement gap.

## DISCUSSION QUESTIONS

1. How are we ensuring that the Home Language Survey is administered consistently and that parents are appropriately equipped to complete it accurately?

2. How are we ensuring that English learners are placed in the appropriate language proficiency level? Do we have a small-scale internal assessment that we can use to periodically measure English language proficiency, in between annual administrations of the state language proficiency assessment?

3. How are content teachers in our school/district currently assessing English learners? If we are not using the student's primary language, then how are we ensuring that we are getting an accurate picture of the student's content knowledge?

4. Are teachers in our school/district open to learning a process for differentiating common formative assessments, particularly for students in the beginning levels of language acquisition? If not, what is/are the obstacle(s)? Is there a team of teachers that would be willing to give the process a try?

# CHAPTER 5

# Challenges in Assessing English Language Learners

Teaching English learners and helping them access the content is a challenge in itself. Assessing English learners presents us with a whole new set of challenges. One of the greatest challenges we have to contend with is the often pronounced achievement gap between our English learners and native English speakers. Abedi and Dietel write that although federal educational mandates, such as No Child Left Behind, strive to establish high expectations for all students and seek to reduce the achievement gap, these worthy goals require extraordinary improvement in student learning (2004). The type of improvement required to meet such high goals requires us to first address the many challenges involved in assessing English learners. These challenges include:

- Historically low ELL performance and slow improvement. Large-scale assessments such as the National Assessment of Educational Progress (NAEP) show that English learners perform far below their native English-speaking peers, and as we saw in Chapter 4, have shown little improvement over many years.

- Measurement accuracy. CRESST research shows that the language demands of assessments negatively influence accurate measurement of ELL performance. If, for example, the teacher focuses on language usage, students may score low when in fact they know the content but may not be able to communicate their knowledge on an assessment that has not been modified.

- Instability of the subgroup. Reclassifying, or redesignating, high-performing ELL students as language proficient results in a "treadmill" effect in which ELL high achievers exit the English learner subgroup and are replaced by new English learners. Consequentially, this results in a downward trend in ELL test scores worsened by the addition of new ELL students, who are typically low achieving. (Abedi and Dietel, 2004)

Although there appear to be some glimmers of hope reflected on some state assessments, overall English learner performance on assessments lags far behind that of their native English-speaking peers. So how can we begin to tackle some of these challenges?

## MEETING THE CHALLENGES

CRESST research has shown that modifying the language of test questions increases ELL performance, frequently by as much as 10 to 20 percent (Abedi and Dietel, 2004). This positive effect has been replicated for content-based tests in different subject areas, including mathematics and science. Research such as this confirms that modifying, or differentiating, the language demands of a common formative assessment yields positive effects for English learners. The key is ensuring that in modifying the language we don't diminish the rigor of the task. The charts of Bloom's levels aligned to levels of language acquisition in the Assessment Matrices in Chapter 7 will help teachers ensure that they are maintaining the appropriate level of cognition by choosing verbs appropriate to the language proficiency level of the student.

## WHAT CONSTITUTES APPROPRIATE DIFFERENTIATION OF AN ASSESSMENT?

While much research needs to be done in terms of how large-scale external assessments should be differentiated, we can explore appropriate modifications based upon the research that currently exists. While it would not be appropriate to extrapolate too much from the research since it applies to large-scale external summative assessments and we are planning small-scale internal formative assessments, it does provide us with some insights that would be helpful, particularly in the planning stages. Current research suggests the following guidelines:

- Know your English learner population. As discussed in Chapter 1, knowing the characteristics of a school's or district's specific English learner population is imperative. Such characteristics include country of origin, primary language, years in school in country of birth, years of schooling in the United States, parental education level, proficiency in primary language, and so on. Ideally, this information would be readily available to teachers in a database or housed in the student information system so that any teacher who has an English learner in his classroom can easily access the information. This information is critical in planning both instruction and assessment for English learners. Chapter 6 contains ideas on creating a school database containing critical information for the classroom teacher of every English learner.

- Know the native language proficiency as well as the English proficiency. It is important when planning assessment modifications to understand language proficiency levels. It can help teachers determine whether an accommodation as basic as primary language support would be helpful to a student. While it makes sense that this would be a useful accommodation for all English learners, it would not be helpful to English learners who are not proficient in their primary language. This is an example of how general modifications aren't always appropriate for all students.

- Specify which accommodations or modifications will be allowed. Schools and districts should likewise have policies and guidelines in place that clearly inform teachers about the modifications that are permissible for English learners.

- Clearly define what each accommodation means and entails. Schools and districts should not just name the accommodation or modification but should also clearly define each and provide examples of what the modification looks like (Bachman, et al., 2008).

While it makes sense that states would need such guidelines when administering any large-scale external assessments with modifications, it is also clear that such guidelines are critical for schools and districts when planning and administering small-scale internal common formative assessments. Exhibit 5.1 is an example of state accommodation guidelines that can serve as a model for schools and districts when building their own accommodation guidelines. Likewise, classroom teachers should work with their PLCs to discuss the accommodations that will be made and to ensure that those accommodations are being applied consistently throughout the grade level.

## ANALYZING THE RESULTS

Another reason schools and districts need clearly defined guidelines to establish and define appropriate assessment modifications is that such guidelines ensure we have consistent data that can be acted upon. If, instead, each teacher and school is making modifications based on whim, then it is difficult to compare or use data to confirm such things as program efficacy. In other words, inconsistency in implementation and use of modifications can lead to issues with the validity and reliability of the results. This is as true at the classroom level as it is at the state level. Other considerations include:

- Effectiveness and validity based on supporting evidence. Accommodations should be based upon research and evidence of improvement in ELL students' performance on content tests. For example, linguistic modifications of noncontent vocabulary and sentence structure were found to be effective types of accommodations (Abedi and Lord, 2001).

| EXHIBIT 5.1 | Sample State Accommodation Guidelines for English Learners |
| --- | --- |

## LEP/ELL ACCOMMODATIONS CHECKLIST

The accommodations specified below are in keeping with what has been practiced regularly in the classroom when the student receives instruction and takes classroom tests. When completed by the LEP/ELL Committee, this checklist becomes part of the student's LEP Plan.

Name: _____ School: _____ Grade: _____ Year: _____

**A. Scheduling Accommodations.** Test will be administered:

☐ 1. At a time of day most beneficial to student.

☐ 2. In periods of one subtest followed by a break of _____ minutes.

☐ 3. With flexible scheduling.

☐ 4. With other accommodations needed due to the level of language proficiency.

**B. Setting/Administration Accommodations.** Test will be administered:

☐ 1. In a small group.

☐ 2. With student seated in front of classroom.

☐ 3. In a carrel.

☐ 4. With teacher facing student.

☐ 5. By student's ESL teacher.

☐ 6. In ESL classroom.

☐ 7. Individually.

☐ 8. Using interpreter during time oral instruction is given to the student (Interpreter may only interpret directions—interpreter may not clarify or offer interpretation items.)

☐ 9. With other accommodations needed due to the level of language proficiency.

**C. Format and/or Equipment Accommodations.** Test will be administered with:

☐ 1. Templates.

☐ 2. Marker to maintain place.

☐ 3. Noise buffers.

☐ 4. English/native language translation dictionary (word-to-word translation/no definitions).

☐ 5. English/native language electronic translator (word-to-word translation/no definitions).

☐ 6. With other accommodations needed due to the level of proficiency.

- Alignment between ELL students' language proficiency and the accommodation used. Given that linguistic modifications are the most effective type of accommodation, adequate and timely measurement of an ELL student's language proficiency is critical as a basis for selecting appropriate accommodations. This underscores the importance of schools or districts developing local language proficiency assessments that help them to monitor and adjust instruction when the student's language acquisition level changes (see Chapter 4).

- Invariance in the learning target or priority standard to be measured. Accommodations should not alter the learning target(s) measured by the assessment. The type of accommodation used and the way it is implemented should compromise measured learning target(s) as little as possible.

- Access to and familiarity with accommodations. Any and all accommodations should be accessible to all English learners. Accommodation procedures should also be open and transparent, and equally familiar to all test takers (Bachman, et al., 2008).

Ensuring that these points have been considered helps teachers trust that the results from common formative assessments are valid and reliable. Additionally, if an assessment encompasses a performance task or constructed-response items that require a scoring guide, teachers will need to create the scoring guide collaboratively and use it consistently so that they score student work consistently. When scoring and analyzing the work, teachers need to determine what the role of language will be in the scoring criteria. Specifically, do the scoring criteria for content-area assessments focus on the knowledge, skills, and abilities being tested, and not on the quality of the language in which the response is expressed (i.e., are ELLs inappropriately penalized for lacking English language skills)? It is important to make it exceedingly clear to everyone on the team that the focus for English learners is on the content and not on their use of and proficiency in the English language.

## USING THE RESULTS

As discussed in Chapter 3, different assessments have different uses and serve different purposes. One thing we know from the research is that there is no one-size-fits-all assessment that meets all needs. Based on information from available states' documents, many states were found to use their English Language Proficiency test for multiple purposes (e.g., identification, placement, redesignation, diagnostics, and instruction). Unfortunately, many schools and districts have done the same thing. Because they lack individual assessments for all purposes, most end up settling for using the state language proficiency assessment as the default assessment to meet all needs, users, and uses. However, it is important to recognize that a single assessment cannot serve all purposes.

## DOES ASSESSMENT RAISE THE ENGLISH LEARNER'S AFFECTIVE FILTER?

Theories of language acquisition, such as the Natural Approach by Stephen Krashen and Tracy Terrell, propose that English learners learn best when we enable them to acquire a new language in a manner similar to the way they learned their native language, naturally and through regular interaction with others who are already proficient in the language (Krashen and Terrell, 1983).

The Natural Approach theory postulates that in the natural process of language acquisition, students acquire language most effectively when they are provided with comprehensible input in a low-affective-filter environment. The affective filter is described as an imaginary wall that is placed between a second-language learner and language input being received by the learner. If the filter is on, the learner is blocking out input. The filter turns on when anxiety is high, self-esteem is low, or motivation is low. Hence, a low-anxiety setting is best for language acquisition. Overt correction will also raise the affective filter as self-esteem in using the language diminishes. Krashen goes on to state that "the best methods are therefore those that supply 'comprehensible input' in low anxiety situations, containing messages that students really want to hear. These methods do not force early production in the second language, but allow students to produce when they are 'ready,' recognizing that improvement comes from supplying communicative and comprehensible input, and not from forcing and correcting production" (Krashen, 1981, pp. 6–7).

## WHAT IMPLICATIONS DOES THE AFFECTIVE FILTER HAVE FOR ASSESSMENT?

If the assessments students have encountered in the past have mostly been summative in nature, then it's possible they've been perceived as negative experiences resulting in failing grades. In this case, the affective filter has likely been raised, causing students to become anxious and self-conscious. If, instead, we begin to use assessment formatively and students receive useful feedback that helps them see themselves as capable learners, then assessment can become an integral part of the learning process in which students see an opportunity to demonstrate what they have learned. Our challenge as teachers is to change our students' perspective if they've developed a negative view of assessment. Once they learn to trust the formative assessment process, they will begin to see it as an opportunity for success instead of failure.

# CONCLUSION

Challenges abound when it comes to assessing English learners. As we've learned, however, there's a lot that schools and districts can do to ensure that teachers are appropriately differentiating their assessments, including getting to know the English learner population we serve and having an accurate measure of English language proficiency on which to base instructional and assessment decisions. Teachers can use existing research that confirms that the most successful differentiation that can be made for English learners is modifying the language of the assessment. Chapters 6, 7, and 8 will outline a process by which ESL teachers and content or self-contained mainstream teachers can work collaboratively to modify the language and tasks of a common formative assessment, with the result that students are better able to demonstrate their proficiency and teachers are better able to provide students with meaningful feedback.

Source: Alabama Department of Education.

# DISCUSSION QUESTIONS

1. How knowledgeable are we about our English learner population? How do we use the information to help us design appropriate curriculum, instruction, and assessment opportunities?

2. Regarding performance on large-scale external assessments (standardized assessment results and language proficiency assessment results):

    —How have our English learners performed over the last three years?

    —Do the scores accurately portray the performance of our English learners?

    —Do we consider the scores to be accurate measures of content knowledge, or is performance dependent on language proficiency?

    —How do we think the "treadmill" effect has impacted our scores?

3. Regarding performance on small-scale internal assessments (site or classroom assessments):

    —How have our English learners performed over the last three years?

—Do the scores accurately portray the performance of our English learners?

—Do we consider the scores to be accurate measures of content knowledge, or is performance dependent on language proficiency?

—How do we think the "treadmill" effect has impacted our scores?

4. Do we have other language proficiency assessments, in addition to the state English Language Proficiency (ELP) assessment, that help us appropriately differentiate common formative assessments? If not, how can we use the process outlined in Chapter 6 to design our own ELP assessments?

# Formative and Summative Assessment of Language Proficiency for English Learners

## THE STARTING POINT: STATE LANGUAGE PROFICIENCY ASSESSMENTS

As mentioned in Chapter 1, all English learners are assessed annually in the area of language proficiency. Title III of No Child Left Behind requires that these assessments:

- Measure annual progress in English language proficiency in the four domains of Reading, Writing, Listening, and Speaking, with a separate measure for comprehension (Listening and Reading).
- Be aligned to state-developed English Language Proficiency (ELP)/English Language Development (ELD) standards.
- Relate to the state-adopted content standards, including those for reading/ language arts and mathematics. (Abedi, 2007, pp. 6–8)

Typically, there is an oral portion of the assessment that may be administered one on one in addition to a written portion composed of mostly selected- and short-response items. While these assessments provide valuable insights into a student's language proficiency level as of a particular point in time, teachers often receive the scores long after the assessment was administered. Because language acquisition is a fluid process, the assessment results are typically already outdated when they are received. It is important to remember that language acquisition is a developmental process and that language acquisition levels are flexible. McLaughlin and his colleagues (McLaughlin, Blanchard, and Osanai, 1995) very accurately portray the process of acquiring a language as analogous to the actions of waves, "moving in and out, generally moving in one direction, but receding, then moving forward again" (pp. 3–4). For this reason, many teachers don't feel that the state language proficiency assessment results provide accurate information that can be used to inform instruction.

The other issue that hampers the use of state language proficiency assessment results is the fact that most teachers are not made aware of the scores and levels of their English learners. While ESL teachers may receive the results and even use them for grouping purposes, most content-area or self-contained mainstream teachers are either not provided the scores or may receive them and after using them for grouping purposes may feel that they are not useful. If these teachers do receive the scores, they typically will receive only the overall language proficiency level and not the specific scores for the individual domains. This overall score is most commonly used to group students for ESL or ELD instruction. As mentioned in previous chapters, it is the domain-specific scores that are most important instructionally for teachers of any English learner to have.

## KNOWING YOUR POPULATION

Critical to the success of any English learner is the knowledge the classroom teacher has about that student. Specifically, every teacher who has English learners in her classroom should have access to information about her students that she can use to make instructional decisions. In fact, all schools should have an English learner database that houses the information that all ESL, content, *and* self-contained mainstream teachers need to have. The database should contain, at a minimum, the following information:

- Student name
- Years in U.S. schools
- Overall English language proficiency level
- Domain-specific scores for Listening, Speaking, Reading, and Writing
- Primary language spoken
- Years in school prior to arrival in the United States
- Parent education level

Other characteristics that affect the rate of language acquisition and could be added to the database include (Tabors, 1997):

- Age
- Age of arrival in U.S. schools
- Immigration or refugee status
- Rural or urban background
- Proficiency in conversational English
- Proficiency in academic and written English

- Family circumstances and responsibilities
- Living situation
- History of mobility
- Employment and work schedule
- Trauma
- Family legal status
- Family educational history
- Birth order in the family
- Religious beliefs and practices
- Continued contact with country of origin and language
- Gender roles and assumptions
- Aspirations and expectations
- Interests, talents, and skills

While it would be impossible to include all of the information listed above, each school should decide, based upon its specific population, what information will be included in the database. Additionally, teachers need professional development regarding the use of the information and scores in planning appropriate instructional and assessment opportunities for ELLs.

## THE CASE FOR ESL TEACHERS TO CONDUCT PERIODIC LANGUAGE PROFICIENCY ASSESSMENTS

It is highly recommended that in addition to the state's large-scale annual assessment, ESL teachers conduct their own progress monitoring of each ELL's language proficiency levels on an ongoing basis. The purpose of this assessment is to provide the ESL and mainstream classroom teachers with the most accurate information about a student's language proficiency levels so that appropriate instruction can be planned that will help the student reach the next level of language acquisition. Because of the fluidity of language acquisition, these periodic language proficiency assessments help the ESL and content or self-contained teachers plan lessons that are reflective of a student's true and accurate language proficiency levels. While levels in the domains may not change significantly, any minor change in any one of the domains could mean a difference in the instruction that the student receives. You might be wondering just how useful periodic assessment of language proficiency would be to teachers. Let's take a look at the following English learner profile to see.

|  | **Trimester 1** | **Trimester 2** | **Trimester 3** |
|---|---|---|---|
| Reading Level | 3 | 3 | 4 |
| Writing Level | 2 | 2 | 3 |
| Listening Level | 3 | 3 | 3 |
| Speaking Level | 4 | 4 | 5 |
| Overall Level | **3** | **3** | **4** |

First of all, the profile shows that the English learner has made progress in three domains, Reading, Writing, and Speaking. These scores were determined by a small-scale internal common assessment of language proficiency. This team of teachers administers their own language proficiency measure, in addition to the state English Language Proficiency assessment, three times per year and shares the results with content or self-contained mainstream teachers. While the results of the state assessment may have provided a good starting point, the results of the small-scale internal language proficiency assessments administered during the course of the year are essential if teachers are to plan lessons and assessments that align with a student's true level of language proficiency. In this example, both ESL and content or self-contained mainstream teachers would take note of the fact that in the third trimester this student reached Level 4 in Reading, Level 3 in Writing, and Level 5 in Speaking. This information would greatly impact the instruction planned for this student. For example:

- The student has reached near-native proficiency in Speaking and is ready to complete all of the assignments that involve speaking that a native English speaker would complete.

- The student's proficiency in Reading has improved from Level 3 to Level 4. The student will now be expected to read text and comprehend it at a higher level than had previously been the case. This student may no longer need to read low-readability text that had been provided as a temporary scaffold.

- In Writing, the student has improved from a Level 2 to a Level 3. Temporary scaffolds, such as sentence starters, may gradually be removed since the student's ability to string sentences together has improved.

This example clearly illustrates the need for periodic language proficiency assessments for English learners and exemplifies how the results of these periodic internal assessments would greatly assist both ESL and content or self-contained mainstream teachers in planning appropriate instructional lessons as well as differentiated assessments.

## THE PROCESS: CREATING PERIODIC INTERNAL LANGUAGE PROFICIENCY ASSESSMENTS

In addition to mandating the development of large-scale external language proficiency assessments, Title III also requires states to develop their own set of language proficiency standards. ESL or ELD teachers should be using these standards as the basis for their ESL or ELD instruction. However, it takes more than merely distributing the standards to teachers. According to the work of experts in the field of standards such as Larry Ainsworth, teachers need to know and understand their standards thoroughly in order to teach and assess them effectively (2003). After identifying the prioritized list of language proficiency standards, teachers must "unwrap" the standards to truly get at the essence of what the standards are requiring us to teach.

The first step is for ESL/ELD teachers to work collaboratively on the process of defining what it is they are assessing as well as the purpose of their assessment. We will now take a look at the 12 steps to creating an assessment from the perspective of an ESL teacher, which were previewed in Chapter 3. The first five steps help teams of ESL teachers clearly answer the question, Assess what?, while a discussion about how the results will be used (Assess why?) helps to clarify whether the purpose is summative or formative.

**Step 1: Identify the Prioritized Language Proficiency Standards to be taught in the Unit of Instruction.** Using the language proficiency standards for your state, identify the prioritized language proficiency standards that are to be taught within the ESL unit of instruction. Use the following criteria:

> **Endurance (Life):** Is this standard a life skill that students will use in their everyday lives?
>
> **Leverage (Tests):** Is this standard assessed on the state language proficiency assessment?
>
> **Readiness (School):** Is this standard a prerequisite skill for language learning that will take place in school in years to come?

Ideally, ESL teachers should be working in concert with content teachers to either frontload the content they will be learning or provide English learners with additional opportunities to engage with the content. If this is the model that your school site is using, it would be appropriate to include prioritized content standards within the unit of instruction. In this way, language is taught within the context of content and not in isolation.

**Step 2: "Unwrap" Language Proficiency Standards.** "Unwrap" the language proficiency standards as well as any applicable supporting content standards into skills and concepts. Use Bloom's Taxonomy to identify the cognitive levels of the skills listed in the standards. What does "unwrapping" look like? Let's take a look at the following English language proficiency standard:

> IDENTIFY using key words or pictures the <u>basic sequence of events in stories read aloud</u>.

"Unwrapping" the standard involves capitalizing or circling the verbs and underlining the nouns or noun phrases. The verbs are then cross-referenced with Bloom's Taxonomy to inform us of the level of rigor of the standard.

**Step 3: Create a Graphic Organizer.** Create a graphic organizer that makes sense to you and your team. The graphic organizer should include the skills, concepts, and Bloom's levels. Using the standard in Step 2, let's take a look at the "unwrapped" standard and Bloom's level as represented in a graphic organizer:

> (2) IDENTIFY (basic sequence of events in stories read aloud, *using key words or pictures*)

When instructing groups of teachers in this process, they will often comment that they would much rather teach from the "unwrapped" standard than from the actual standard because the "unwrapped" standard contains at a glance all the information a teacher needs to plan appropriate instruction and assessment.

**Step 4: Determine the Big Ideas.** Determine Big Ideas only *if* you've created a language proficiency assessment that is interdisciplinary and contains content area standard(s) in addition to the language proficiency standards. When writing a Big Idea, think, "What is it I want my English learners to remember about the content long after the instruction is over?" Writing Big Ideas and Essential Questions for your prioritized language proficiency standards is very illuminating and beneficial to ESL teachers. It helps focus assessment and instruction on profound understanding, or the "deep end of the pool," versus focusing on strings of isolated facts.

**Step 5: Write Essential Questions.** Write student-friendly Essential Questions that will pique students' interest and compel them to learn the content. Essential

Questions should be written in student-friendly terms, and should therefore be written for each level of language proficiency.

The next seven steps in the process help define the bigger question, Assess how? Again, we will take a look at the steps from the perspective of the ESL teacher.

**Step 6: Review and evaluate the different types of assessment formats and item types.** Consider the Bloom's levels and any "unwrapped" content standards that may be assessed in conjunction with the "unwrapped" language proficiency standards. Remember that any language proficiency assessment must use the four domains of language as a vehicle for assessing.

**Step 7: Select the assessment item types that will provide the most credible evidence that the student has mastered the "unwrapped" concepts and skills, or learning targets.** Which items on the language proficiency assessment can be assessed with selected-response items? Constructed-response items? Performance-based items?

**Step 8: Collaboratively create the pre- and post-assessment items.** Once the assessment blueprint has been created, it is time to create the assessment. Decide whether the pre-assessment can also be used as the post-assessment or whether minor adjustments might need to be made. Ideally, it is best to keep the pre- and post-assessments the same. If there is too much variation between the pre- and post-assessment items, a valid comparison cannot be made and growth cannot be determined.

**Step 9: Administer the common formative language proficiency pre-assessment, score and analyze the results collaboratively.** Collaborative scoring, particularly of items that require a scoring guide, is important for teachers as it assists them in clearly defining proficiency and ensures that the scoring guide is being applied consistently. In this way, teachers can be confident that a paper they've rated as proficient would also have been rated proficient by their colleagues. There is no better way for teachers to achieve inter-rater reliability of scores and to continuously adjust their scoring so that they are all defining proficiency in the same way. Professional development in the creation and use of scoring guides and in collaboratively scoring student work is critical to this process (Ainsworth and Viegut, 2006, p. 66). Based upon the grade-level appropriateness, teachers decide how best to share assessment results with students. Providing students with an opportunity to reflect upon their performance and then set personal goals for improvement helps engage students in the assessment process and becomes highly motivating when they see their growth after the administration of the post-assessment.

**Step 10: Using the pre-assessment results, plan daily lessons and learning activities that will get students to master the "unwrapped" concepts and skills.** ESL teachers will analyze the results of the assessment within their Data Teams and determine the students who are:

1. Proficient,

2. Close to proficient,

3. Far to go, or

4. In need of intensive support.

Identifying these distinct and focused groups for each level of language proficiency will help drive instruction that is directly tied to student needs. This is where differentiated instruction is born! Teachers work together to answer questions such as, "How will we meet the needs of students not yet proficient as well as the needs of students who are proficient prior to any instruction?" ESL teachers determine the research-based strategies that will be used to teach the standards to all students and ensure that every teacher on the team is clear about how the strategies are to be implemented.

**Step 11: Teach the unit, formatively assess during the course of the unit, and continue using differentiated instructional strategies to meet the needs of English learners at all levels.** The instruction cycle commences, and teachers use classroom-based formative assessments, such as exit-slips, to continue to provide diagnostic feedback to English learners. Strategies are modified if the team determines that the strategies are not yielding the expected results.

**Step 12: Administer the common formative language proficiency post-assessment.** The Data Team meets again to determine whether students in each of the categories—including English learners already proficient, close to proficient, far to go, and in need of intensive support—experienced growth as a result of instruction. Are any students still not proficient? If so, why are they not proficient? What targeted intervention can we provide? When? For how long?

## WHAT NEXT?
## HOW DO WE BEGIN THE PROCESS?

As recommended by Ainsworth and Viegut in *Common Formative Assessments,* it is always best to begin with a team of teachers who are ready and willing to move in this direction. Providing some form of professional development for the team is essential in ensuring that they feel equipped with the tools and strategies to be successful. The team can then begin by making important decisions, such as how many times they will administer a common formative language proficiency assessment. In the example shared earlier in this chapter, the ESL team decided on three administrations, once per trimester. The team could then begin the twelve-step process as outlined in the previous paragraphs. Important considerations for leaders include:

- Providing collaboration time for teams of teachers to work on the development of high-quality common formative language proficiency assessments.

- Ensuring that the master schedule is created with opportunities for teacher collaboration in mind.

- Scheduling a meeting time with the ESL team to discuss their action plan and to be made aware of any assistance the team may require.

- Ensuring that appropriate professional development is provided at key points in the year when the team determines it would be most helpful to them. (Adapted from Ainsworth and Viegut, 2006, p. 75)

## RESOURCES—SAMPLE FORMATIVE LANGUAGE PROFICIENCY ASSESSMENTS

Grade-level teams can develop an Assessment Blueprint that helps in the planning stages of the assessment. In the sample Assessment Blueprints on the next few pages, the prioritized language proficiency standards are shown in **bold** type and any supporting standards are shown in regular type. The "unwrapped" standard appears below the text of each standard, and includes the Bloom's Taxonomy level in parentheses.

### K–2 Samples

Exhibit 6.1 is a blueprint for a K–2, Level 1 Pre-Production language proficiency assessment. Because the assessment is designed for K–2 students in Level 1 of language proficiency, it is a performance-based assessment.

Exhibit 6.2 is a blueprint for a K–2, Level 4 Early Advanced language proficiency assessment. Note that as we move up in language proficiency levels, there are more paper-and-pencil items in the assessment. However, because the assessment is for the K–2 grade span, a significant portion of the assessment is still performance based.

Both samples make use of content learned through the reading of *The Rainbow Fish*; however, we even see content included in the language proficiency standard in the Early Advanced writing sample. In this way, when teachers plan the instruction that prepares students for this language proficiency assessment, they will plan lessons that contain both content and language objectives.

**EXHIBIT 6.1**

# K–2 Level 1: Pre-Production—Assessment Blueprint

|  | **Listening and Speaking** | **Reading** | **Writing** |
|---|---|---|---|
| **ELP Standards** | Respond to simple directions and questions using physical actions and other means of non-verbal communication. **LS-3**<br><br>Begin to speak with a few words or sentences using some English phonemes and rudimentary English grammatical forms. **LS-1**<br><br>(3) RESPOND (to simple directions and questions *using physical actions*)<br><br>(3) RESPOND (to simple directions and questions *using nonverbal communication*)<br><br>(2) SPEAK (using some English phonemes and rudimentary grammatical forms) | Respond orally to stories read aloud, using physical actions and other means of nonverbal communication. **RC-1**<br><br>Identify using key words or pictures the basic sequence of events in stories read aloud. **RC-5**<br><br>(3) RESPOND (orally to stories read aloud, *using actions and other nonverbal communication*)<br><br>(2) IDENTIFY (basic sequence of events in stories read aloud, *using key words or pictures*) | Write a few words or phrases about an event or character from a story read aloud by the teacher. **WS-3**<br><br>Copy the English alphabet legibly. **WS-1**<br><br>Copy words posted and commonly used in the classroom. **WS-2**<br><br>(4) WRITE (about an event or character, *using a few words or phrases*)<br><br>(1) COPY (alphabet legibly)<br><br>(1) COPY (words posted and commonly used in the classroom) |
| **Performance Tasks** | *After multiple experiences with the reading of *The Rainbow Fish*, ask the following questions:<br>1. Point to a fish. **LS-3**<br>2. What is the name of the fish in the story?  Point to the name of the fish. **LS-3, LS-1**<br>3. Show me what the fish did. **LS-3**<br>4. Tell me what the fish did. **LS-1**<br>5. Point to the word that tells what Rainbow Fish did. **LS-3, LS-1** | *Picture walk<br>*Key Vocabulary Prediction with a picture card deck to predict what the story might be about.<br>*Multiple experiences with the reading of *The Rainbow Fish*. Teacher reads story and uses realia and TPR to act out story.<br>1. Using picture cards with scenes from the story, ask student to properly sequence the major events. **RC-5**<br>2. Student will respond to the story using physical actions or other means of nonverbal communication. (Point to the rainbow fish, etc.) **RC-1**<br>3. After sharing the word bank, use word cards and ask student to point to the following words: **(RC-1, RC-5)**<br>coral (cognate)<br>in<br>and<br>ocean | *After multiple experiences with *The Rainbow Fish*, direct student to do the following tasks (use TPR strategies to ensure that students fully comprehend the task):<br>Draw a picture of Rainbow Fish showing what happened in the story. Show me where Rainbow fish lives and include some of the characters in your drawing. Tell me who is in your picture. Using the word bank, write a few words that describe your drawing. Label your picture also using words from the word bank.  **(WS-3, WS-1, WS-2)**<br><br>**Scoring Guide:**<br>**Mastery—**<br>—Student uses words from the word bank or from the classroom word wall to describe the drawing. (WS-2, **WS-3**)<br>—Student labels the picture correctly, writing legibly and using words from the word bank. (WS-1, WS-2)<br><br>**Approaching—**<br>—Meets two of the Mastery criteria<br><br>**Beginning—**<br>—Meets fewer than two of the Mastery criteria |

| EXHIBIT 6.2 | K–2 Level 4: Early Advanced—Assessment Blueprint |
| --- | --- |

| | Listening and Speaking | Reading | Writing |
| --- | --- | --- | --- |
| **ELP Standards** | Listen attentively to stories/information, and orally identify key details and concepts. **LS-1**<br><br>Make oneself understood when speaking, using consistent standard English grammatical forms, sounds, intonation, pitch, and modulation, but may have random errors. **LS-3**<br><br>(3) LISTEN (attentively to stories/information)<br><br>(1) IDENTIFY (key details, concepts, *orally*)<br><br>(2) SPEAK (using consistent standard English grammatical forms, sounds, intonations, pitch, and modulation) | Read stories and texts from content areas and orally respond to them by restating facts and details to clarify ideas. **RC-5**<br><br>Read text and use detailed sentences to identify orally the main idea and use the idea to draw inferences about the text. **RC-1**<br><br>(3) READ (stories and texts from content areas)<br><br>(3) RESPOND (to stories by restating facts and details)<br><br>(3) READ (text)<br><br>(2) IDENTIFY (main ideas and use ideas to draw inferences) | Writes short narratives that include elements of setting, characters, and events. **WS-1**<br><br>Uses complex vocabulary & sentences appropriate for language arts & other content areas (e.g., math, science, social studies). **WS-3**<br><br>(5) WRITE (short narratives that include elements of setting, characters, and events)<br><br>(2) USE (complex vocabulary & sentences appropriate for language arts & other content areas) |
| **Assessment Tasks** | *After multiple experiences with the reading of *The Rainbow Fish*, ask the following questions:<br>1. Can you show me who the main character of the story is? **LS-1**<br>2. What is the name of the main character? **LS-1, LS-3**<br>3. Why did the Rainbow Fish decide to share his scales? **LS-1, LS-3** | *Picture walk<br>*Key Vocabulary Prediction with a picture card deck to predict what the story might be about.<br>*Multiple experiences with the reading of *The Rainbow Fish*. Student reads story<br>1. Ask the student to use facts and details from the story to complete a story map. **RC-5**<br>2. Student is asked to respond to the following questions:<br>What lesson did the Rainbow Fish learn? How do you know? **RC-1** | *After reading The Rainbow Fish, direct student to complete the following task:<br>Think about what just happened in the story, *The Rainbow Fish*. Draw a picture showing where it happened, what happened, and who was there. Then, write a few sentences telling me about the story. Describe the setting, characters, and events in your picture. Remember to use the ocean vocabulary we've been learning about.<br><br>**Scoring Guide:**<br>**Mastery—**<br>—Student writes a short narrative. (**WS-1**, WS-3)<br>—The narrative includes a setting<br>—The narrative includes characters } (WS-1, WS-3)<br>—The narrative includes events<br>—Student uses appropriate ocean vocabulary to describe the setting. (WS-3)<br>**Approaching—**<br>—Meets three of the Mastery criteria<br>**Beginning—**<br>—Meets fewer than three of the Mastery criteria |

| EXHIBIT 6.3 | Grades 6–8 Level 2: Early Production—Assessment Blueprint |
| --- | --- |

| | Listening and Speaking | Reading | Writing |
| --- | --- | --- | --- |
| **ELP Standards** | Ask and answer questions by using phrases or simple sentences. LS-2<br><br>Begin to be understood when speaking but may have some inconsistent use of standard English grammatical forms and sounds (e.g., plurals, simple past tense, pronouns such as he or she). LS-1<br><br>(3) ASK (questions using phrases or simple sentences)<br><br>(4) ANSWER (questions using phrases or simple sentences)<br><br>(2) SPEAK (using standard English grammatical forms and sounds) | Read text and orally identify the main ideas and details of informational materials, literary text, and text in content areas by using simple sentences. RC-4<br><br>(3) READ (text—informational materials, literary text, text in content areas)<br><br>(1) IDENTIFY (main ideas, and details, *orally*) | Write expository compositions, such as descriptions, comparison and contrast, and problem and solution, that include a main idea and some details in simple sentences. WS-5<br><br>(5) WRITE (expository compositions)<br>Include<br>• Main idea<br>• Details |
| **Assessment Tasks** | *After multiple experiences with the reading of *The Adventures of Tom Sawyer* (using modified low-readability text), ask the following questions:<br><br>1. Using the picture cards, can you show me who the main characters of the story are? **LS-2**<br><br>2. What are the names of the main characters? **LS-2, LS-1**<br><br>3. What is a question you would ask Tom Sawyer about Becky? **LS-2, LS-1** | * Student reads *The Adventures of Tom Sawyer* (using modified low-readability text).<br><br>1. Ask the student to orally read the following passage: **RC-4**<br>"He had had a nice, good, idle time all the while—plenty of company—and the fence had three coats of whitewash on it! If he hadn't run out of whitewash he would have bankrupted every boy in the village."<br><br>2. Tell me about this part of the story. How does Tom get his friends to whitewash the fence for him? | *After reading *The Adventures of Tom Sawyer*, direct student to complete the following task:<br><br>Think about the events you read about in the story, *The Adventures of Tom Sawyer*. Tom experienced lots of adventures. Write about a time you had an adventure. Draw a picture showing where it happened, what happened, and who was there. Then, write a few sentences describing your adventure. Describe the setting, characters, and events in your picture.<br><br>**Scoring Guide:**<br><br>**Mastery—**<br>—Student writes a descriptive composition. **(WS-5)**<br>—The student describes<br>—The setting<br>—The characters } **(WS-5)**<br>—The events<br>—Student writes using simple sentences. **(WS-5)**<br><br>**Approaching—**<br>—Meets three of the Mastery criteria<br><br>**Beginning—**<br>—Meets fewer than three of the Mastery criteria |

## Grades 6–8 Sample

Exhibit 6.3 is a blueprint for a grade 6–8, Level 2 Early Production language proficiency assessment. Note how the connection to content areas is more pronounced at these grade levels than at the K–2 grade levels. Again, this reinforces the importance of teaching language within the context of content, and also makes for a much richer language proficiency assessment.

# CONCLUSION

The creation of periodic language proficiency assessments by ESL teachers is a necessary element in educating English learners. Because state language proficiency assessments are administered only once per year and the results are usually not received in a timely manner, these assessments are useful as accountability tools, and perhaps even as wise initial measures on which to base the grouping of English learners for ESL instruction. However, these characteristics are precisely what make the results unusable for instructional use by either the ESL or the content/self-contained classroom teacher. For this purpose, teachers need the results of small-scale internal langauge proficiency assessments created thoughtfully by teams of ESL teachers who understand the needs of their particular ELL population. By following the twelve-step process outlined in this chapter, teachers can create well-aligned, timely, and accurate language proficiency assessments that will yield valuable instructional data that both the ESL and content-area or self-contained mainstream teachers can use to plan both differentiated instruction and assessments.

## DISCUSSION QUESTIONS

1. What assessment measure is used at your school/district for grouping English learners for ESL instruction? Do English learners remain in the same groups all year long? If so, does the following English learner profile cause you to question this decision?

|  | Trimester 1 | Trimester 2 | Trimester 3 |
|---|---|---|---|
| Reading Level | 3 | 3 | 4 |
| Writing Level | 2 | 2 | 3 |
| Listening Level | 3 | 3 | 3 |
| Speaking Level | 4 | 4 | 5 |
| Overall Level | **3** | **3** | **4** |

2. What assessment measures are shared with content or self-contained mainstream classroom teachers about their English learners? Other than the state language proficiency assessment results, what other measures can these teachers use during the course of the year to help them provide appropriately differentiated instruction that matches the true language proficiency levels of English learners? Is there a team of ESL/ELD teachers who would be willing to pilot this process? How can they be supported?

3. Is there an English learner database that can be shared with all teachers who teach English learners during the course of the day? If not, would someone on your team be willing to develop one? Carefully consider what information would be most useful to include in the database based upon the characteristics of your English learner population. Use the resources in this chapter to help you.

# CHAPTER 7

# Formative and Summative Assessment of Content Knowledge for English Learners

Content-area and self-contained mainstream teachers face many unique challenges when assessing English learners. Most of these teachers teach in classrooms where students range from English learners to native English speakers, and from high achieving to learning disabled. Despite our best intentions, it is challenging to be aware of the needs of all students at any point in time. Resources such as an English learner database (see Chapter 6) would inform content-area or self-contained teachers of such things as ELL English acquisition levels. In fact, if you are a content-area or self-contained mainstream teacher, you may not currently be aware of all of the language acquisition levels of the ELLs in your classroom. If so, you are not alone. In my conversations with teachers across the country, I have found that it is not even unusual for content or self-contained mainstream teachers to be unaware of the identities of the English learners sitting in their classrooms. How can this be? If there is one thing I understand intimately about being a classroom teacher, it is that it can be an incredibly overwhelming job. We are constantly being presented with new responsibilities and new initiatives that oftentimes take our focus off of what matters most—instruction. For those old enough to remember the *I Love Lucy* episode in which Lucy is working at a factory and can't seem to keep up with the conveyor belt because of the unreasonably quick pace at which it is moving, I wonder if you've ever felt as she did—no matter how fast you move, it seems that the conveyor belt is always at least one step ahead of you.

While watching this scenario play out in black and white is quite humorous, living in a similar scenario every day in your classroom is no laughing matter! Teachers are feeling more fractured and overburdened than ever before. Our first step, as mentioned previously, is to begin by taking stock of current initiatives. Those that are having a direct impact on student achievement should be continued, but those that are not should be taken off the plates of busy teachers and administrators.

While many of the initiatives may in fact be worthwhile, the sheer volume of them makes their implementation highly unlikely. Yet, we march on, hoping that each new initiative may hold the answer to increased performance for our lowest-performing students. Sadly, what we typically find is that each new initiative has no greater impact than the last. And because we are implementing so many simultaneously, it is hard to know which initiative, if any, is responsible for the results we are getting. What research has shown is that it is not so much the initiatives, but rather the degree of implementation that matters most (Reeves, 2010).

When it comes to common formative assessments, most teams of content or self-contained mainstream teachers will say that they are currently using them in their classrooms. If you are one of those teams, ask yourself the following questions:

1. Did we begin by identifying priority standards for our content area? Did we use the following criteria to identify the priorities:

   **Endurance (Life):** Is this standard a life skill that students will use in their everyday lives?

   **Leverage (Test):** Is this standard assessed on the state assessment?

   **Readiness (School):** Is this standard a prerequisite skill for content learning that will take place in years to come?

2. Did we "unwrap" the standard(s) into the component concepts and skills along with Bloom's Taxonomy levels?

3. Did we take into consideration the purpose for our assessment? Is it meant to take place at the end of learning to help us determine whether our students have met the standard(s) (**summative assessment**)? Is it meant to take place while the learning is happening to help us provide formative feedback to our students so that they can see the gap between where they are and where they need to be, as well as the steps they can take to close the gap (**formative assessment**)? Will the results provide feedback to us that will help us refine, adjust, and focus our instruction?

4. Will we use Data Teams or another data analysis protocol to analyze the results of the assessment? Will the analysis process involve identifying where each student is in relation to the target and then identifying the research-based strategies that will help him reach the target?

If you answered yes to these four questions, then Congratulations! You have fully implemented common formative assessments! If you answered yes to one, two, or three of the questions, then Congratulations! You've begun the process. You've tackled the most difficult challenge, which is getting started. Now it's just a matter of identifying where you are in the process and moving to the next step. If you answered no to all four questions, then Congratulations! You are reading this book, which means you are open to learning more about the process, and what's more, you've made it to Chapter 7, which means you've stuck with the process this far! If you did answer no to all the questions, then consider question 5:

> 5. Are we administering an *assessment in common*? In other words, did we all choose to use the same assessment provided with our textbook?

If this sounds like a somewhat accurate description of where your team currently is in their use of common formative assessments, then I'd encourage you to begin by checking for alignment of the items on your assessment (see Chapter 3). Your team may feel more compelled to follow you on this journey if there is a perceived need. Checking for alignment is typically all it takes for teachers to realize that they should at a minimum take a closer look at how well assessments align to the priority standards. It is also frustrating to realize the countless hours spent scoring those assessments when they may have not been fully aligned to the priority standards and may have been leading to some inaccurate inferences.

## BEGINNING THE PROCESS

Identifying where your content or self-contained team is in the process of implementing common formative assessments is a critical first step in beginning the process of creating common formative assessments for English learners. Because the process for content or self-contained teachers begins with an existing assessment, it is important that that assessment be one of high quality. Although that is the ideal starting point, so critical is the need for English learners, that I would encourage you to begin the process with whatever assessment you are currently using. Oftentimes, this process highlights any items on the original assessment that may need to be altered or removed altogether.

## KNOWING YOUR PURPOSE

In the content or self-contained mainstream teachers' classrooms, it is important to begin the design process by determining the purpose of the assessment. There is no denying that creating differentiated assessments is time intensive. The question we need to consider, however, is how do we determine what our English learners know if we don't differentiate the assessments? In the absence of the detailed and accurate data we would gather from a differentiated assessment, what would we use to help us plan appropriate learning activities? If ensuring learning for all students is our goal, then we can't afford to not differentiate assessments for English learners.

While differentiation takes time, the cost of not doing it is too great. It bears stating that without appropriate differentiation, assessment results will be inaccurate, at best. Larry Ainsworth and Donald Viegut, in their book *Common Formative Assessments*, write about how assessments help teachers make inferences about student achievement (2006). If the assessments are not well aligned, then it's fair to say that our inferences will be invalid and thus the instructional decisions we make based upon those inferences may not reflect the true needs of the student, with the implication that the inferences we make are only as good as the measures on which we base them. As we have seen in past chapters, invalid inferences could have detrimental effects on the success of English learners in our school systems.

## WHAT YOU NEED TO KNOW

The typical English language learner will develop Basic Interpersonal Communication Skills (BICS) in about one to two years. This means that you may not be able to distinguish the English learners in your classroom just by listening to them. In fact, it is possible that some ELLs in your room have reached Level 3, Speech Emergence, or even higher in the domain of Speaking. ELLs who have reached Level 3 have developed strong BICS and social vocabulary and may sound proficient to you. You may assume that these students comprehend classroom activities, your lectures, and the textbook, when, in fact, they do not. Keep in mind that while ELLs may be assigned an overall level, they may be at different levels of language acquisition in different domains. If your school does not have an English learner database that contains profile information for your ELLs, you may need to talk to the ESL/ELD teacher at your site to ascertain the levels of your ELLs in each of the domains. See Chapter 6 for more information on what to include in your English learner database.

Cognitive Academic Language Proficiency (CALP) takes between five and seven years to develop. It may take longer depending upon several factors, including the number of years the child attended school in their native country. As previously mentioned, those students who arrive between the ages of eight and 11 and who attended school prior to arriving in the United States will not only acquire CALP at a faster rate, but will also progress through the levels of language acquisition more quickly. Those students in your mainstream classroom who have limited prior educational experience may take as long as seven to 10 years to acquire CALP. It is precisely the cognitive academic language that helps students successfully learn in the content areas. If they lack the cognitive language, then their language proficiency level in Reading and Writing may be much lower than in Speaking and Listening. This may explain why some of your English learners are struggling to learn the content.

## THE BOTTOM LINE

Getting to know your English learner population as much as possible will help you to plan appropriate instruction and assessments. If you do not have language proficiency information for your English learners, here is what you need to request:

1. Results of the annual state language proficiency assessment. Typically, teachers receive the overall language proficiency levels.

2. Scores for each of the language domains: Listening, Speaking, Reading, and Writing.

You may also want to schedule some time to meet with the ESL teacher or ELL coordinator. If your school site is implementing Professional Learning Communities, talk to your administrator about providing some time for ESL teachers and mainstream teachers to collaborate.

## THE DESIGN PROCESS

We will begin the design process with the creation of the common formative assessment for assessing the content. Once the assessment has been created, we can begin the differentiation process for English learners at the earliest levels of language acquisition. The design process for the common formative assessment for English learners is embedded in the process for native English speakers. The differentiation process for ELLs does not begin until Step 8.

**Step 1: Identify the Prioritized Content Standards to be taught in the Unit of Instruction.** Determine the standards in the unit that are considered nonnegotiable. Use the following criteria:

**Endurance:** Is this standard a life skill that students will use in their everyday lives?

**Leverage:** Is this standard assessed on the state assessment?

**Readiness:** Is this standard a prerequisite skill for content learning that will take place in years to come?

Oftentimes, even after applying the three criteria, teachers will struggle to identify a standard as a priority standard versus a supporting standard. In that case I will ask them, "Is this a standard for which you would put a student into intervention?"

If the answer is yes and the standard meets the other three criteria, then you've found a priority standard.

**Step 2: "Unwrap" the Prioritized Standards.** "Unwrap" the content standards into the concepts and skills. Circle or capitalize the verbs and underline the nouns or noun phrases in the standard. Use Bloom's Taxonomy to determine the level of rigor of the verbs.

> Common Core English Language Arts Writing Standard:
>
> W.2.3 WRITE narratives in which they RECOUNT a well-elaborated event or short sequence of events, INCLUDE details to describe actions, thoughts, and feelings, USE temporal words to signal event order and PROVIDE a sense of closure.

**Step 3: Create a Graphic Organizer.** Display the "unwrapped" standard using a graphic organizer that makes sense to the team. In the example below, the Bloom's Taxonomy level appears in parentheses in front of the verbs.

> (5) WRITE (Narratives)
>
> (2) RECOUNT (Well-elaborated event or short sequence of events)
>
> (2) INCLUDE (Details to describe actions, thoughts, and feelings)
>
> (3) USE (Temporal words to signal event order)
>
> (3) PROVIDE (Sense of closure)

Teachers will often comment that they would much rather teach from the "unwrapped" standard than from the actual standard because the "unwrapped" standard contains at a glance all the information a teacher needs to plan appropriate instruction and assessment.

**Step 4: Determine the Big Ideas.** When writing a Big Idea, think "What is it I want my English learners to remember about the content long after the instruction has ended?" Rather than have students mindlessly memorize facts that are mostly stored in short-term memory, Big Ideas stay with students.

> 1. A narrative is a story, consisting of a series of events where one thing leads to another and at the end you have an outcome.
> 2. The author uses details to describe actions, thoughts, or feelings in a narrative because it helps paint a picture for the reader.

**Step 5: Write Essential Questions.** The Essential Questions are the questions that lead students to the Big Ideas. These will be shared with students, so it is important for teachers to put them into student-friendly language. Notice how the Big Idea is the answer to the Essential Question.

> 1. **What is a narrative? What does a good narrative contain?**
>    A narrative is a story, consisting of a series of events where one thing leads to another and at the end you have an outcome.

2. **Why do authors use detailed descriptions of actions, thoughts, and feelings in a narrative?**

The author uses details to describe actions, thoughts, or feelings in a narrative because it helps paint a picture for the reader.

When content and self-contained mainstream teachers complete the first five design steps, they have defined the Assess what?, which is the first part of the process. Now we go on to the next seven steps, which help us determine the answer to Assess how?

**Step 6: Review and evaluate the different types of assessment formats and item types.** Now that we have defined and narrowed down what we will assess, it is time to determine the best assessment formats and item types to assess the learning targets we've identified in Steps 1–5. We begin by considering the level of rigor of the "unwrapped" standard(s).

**Step 7: Select the assessment item types that will provide the most credible evidence that the student has mastered the "unwrapped" concepts and skills, or learning targets.** Which items on the assessment can be assessed with selected-response items? Constructed-response? Performance-based?

**Step 8: Collaboratively create the pre- and post-assessment items.** Working with our content or grade-level teams, we work on the creation of a common formative pre- and post-assessment. In most cases, it is acceptable to use the same assessment for both pre- and post-assessments.

At this point, we have created the common formative pre- and post-assessments for native English speakers and are ready to create a differentiated version of the assessments, particularly for students at the lower levels of language acquisition.

Using the differentiated verbs and tasks on the Assessment Matrix (see the Assessment Matrices in the Resources section near the end of this chapter), we take each item on the assessment and differentiate it. The Assessment Matrix is an at-a-glance resource for the busy content or self-contained mainstream teacher. Teachers can use the information in the matrix to help them differentiate tasks from an existing common formative assessment.

Column 1 in each matrix contains a general description of the English learner as well as a Bloom's Taxonomy chart containing verbs that are appropriate for a student at that level. There is a broadly held misconception that English learners cannot perform at the higher levels of Bloom's Taxonomy. This chart helps dispel that myth. You will find verbs from the lowest level of Bloom's to the highest level for every language proficiency level. The implication is that even at Level 1, Pre-Production, students can think critically and reason at the highest levels of Bloom's Taxonomy.

Column 2 contains a detailed description of the types of tasks that students at that level of language proficiency can engage in successfully. This column contains tasks in all four domains: Listening, Speaking, Reading, and Writing.

Column 3 provides a description of what teachers can ask of students at that particular level of language proficiency.

It is recommend that teams of teachers use these matrices not only to help them design differentiated assessments, but also to help design differentiated instructional activities.

**Step 8A:** Begin by analyzing the items on the common formative assessment. Which items lend themselves to differentiation for English learners? Some items may not be appropriate, and in that case the Assessment Matrix can be used to help differentiate the item or create a new one.

**Step 8B:** Use the Assessment Matrix to differentiate your assessment. Stay focused on the "unwrapped" standard and Big Ideas. What is it that you want students to know or be able to do? If you get stuck on an item, it may be best to start from scratch and write an item that is better suited to the needs of English learners. Exhibit 7.1 is an example of how the writing standard can be assessed for each level. Native English speakers were asked to:

(5) WRITE (Narratives)

(2) RECOUNT (Well-elaborated event or short sequence of events)

(2) INCLUDE (Details to describe actions, thoughts, and feelings)

(3) USE (Temporal words to signal event order)

(3) PROVIDE (Sense of closure)

1. **What is a narrative? What does a good narrative contain?**

   A narrative is a story, consisting of a series of events where one thing leads to another and at the end you have an outcome.

2. **Why do authors use detailed descriptions of actions, thoughts, and feelings in a narrative?**

   The author uses details to describe actions, thoughts, or feelings in a narrative because it helps paint a picture for the reader.

Notice from Exhibit 7.1 that the greatest amount of differentiation for this task takes place at Levels 1 and 2. Although Level 3 is also slightly differentiated, there is not a very big leap between Level 3 and Levels 4 and 5. Again, a performance-based assessment is used because it is the best match for the type of standard that is being taught.

**Step 9: Administer the common formative pre-assessment, score and analyze the results collaboratively.** Collaborative scoring, particularly of items that require a scoring guide, is important for teachers as it assists them in clearly defining proficiency and ensures that the scoring guide is being applied consistently. In this way, teachers can be confident that a paper they've rated as proficient would also have

| **EXHIBIT 7.1** | **Differentiated Performance-Based Tasks by Language Proficiency Levels** | | | | |
|---|---|---|---|---|---|
| | **Pre-Production** | **Early Production** | **Speech Emergence** | **Intermediate Fluency** | **Advanced Fluency** |
| **Differentiated Assessment Tasks** | *Given a series of familiar scenes, students will use words generated from the Key Vocabulary Prediction, word wall, and word bank to help them complete the Cloze Activity\* describing the events taking place.* | *Given a series of familiar scenes, students will label each scene using words and phrases that narrate what they see happening.* | Students will write a short narrative recounting a series of events. | Students will write a short narrative recounting a series of events that includes elements of setting, character, and events. Students use temporal words and provide a sense of closure. | Students will write a short narrative recounting a series of events that includes elements of setting, character, and events. Students use temporal words and provide a sense of closure. |

\* Cloze Activity—technique in which words are strategically deleted from a passage and replaced with blanks. The passage is presented to students, who insert words as they read the passage to complete and construct meaning from the text.

been rated proficient by their colleagues. There is no better way for teachers to achieve inter-rater reliability of scores and to continuously recalibrate their scoring so that they are all defining proficiency in the same way. Professional development in the creation and use of scoring guides and in collaboratively scoring student work is critical to this process (Ainsworth and Viegut, 2006, p. 66). Depending upon the grade-level appropriateness, teachers decide upon how best to share assessment results with students. Providing students with an opportunity to reflect upon their performance and then set personal goals for improvement helps engage students in the assessment process and becomes highly motivating when they see their growth after the administration of the post-assessment.

**Step 10: Using the pre-assessment results, plan daily lessons and learning activities that will get students to master the "unwrapped" concepts and skills.** Content and self-contained mainstream teachers will analyze the results of the assessment within their Data Teams and determine the students who are

1. Proficient,
2. Close to proficient,
3. Far to go, or
4. In need of intensive support.

These distinct and focused groups for each level of language proficiency will help drive instruction that is directly tied to student needs. This is where differentiated instruction is born! Teachers work together to answer questions such as, "How will we meet the needs of students not yet proficient as well as the needs of students who are proficient prior to any instruction?" Teachers determine the research-based strategies that will be used to teach the standards to all students and ensure that every teacher on the team is clear about how the strategies are to be implemented.

**Step 11: Teach the unit, formatively assess during the course of the unit, and continue using differentiated instructional strategies to make content comprehensible for English learners at all levels.** The instruction cycle commences, and teachers use classroom-based formative assessments, such as exit-slips, to continue to provide diagnostic feedback to all students, including English learners. Strategies are modified if the team determines that a strategy is not yielding the expected results.

**Step 12: Administer the common formative post-assessment.** The Data Team meets again to determine whether students in each of the categories—including English learners already proficient, close to proficient, far to go, and in need of intensive support—experienced growth as a result of instruction. Are any students still not proficient? If so, why are they not proficient? What targeted intervention can we provide? When? For how long?

# RESOURCES—ASSESSMENT MATRICES AND SAMPLE DIFFERENTIATED FORMATIVE ASSESSMENT

| EXHIBIT 7.2 | Assessment Matrix Language Acquisition Level 1: Pre-Production | |
|---|---|---|

| General Description | Students Can | Teacher Should |
|---|---|---|
| Student moves from silent stage with no comprehension to physical responses with minimal comprehension. Student continues to use one- or two-word responses with limited comprehension, and moves to speaking in words and phrases with comprehension of highly contextualized information. | • Respond nonverbally<br>• Respond in simple words and phrases<br>• Respond in L1<br>• Respond physically<br>• Draw<br>• Make connections with prior knowledge<br>• Categorize objects and pictures<br>• Use context to make meaning<br>• Identify people, places, and things<br>• Repeat and recite<br>• Label drawings and diagrams<br>• Describe concrete things, events, places, and people<br>• Explain simple academic concepts<br>• Learn "big ideas" in content areas<br>• Recognize, read basic vocabulary and write words and simple sentences<br>• Listen to simple directions or questions and respond | • Use predictable, patterned text<br>• Use Cloze frames<br>• Ask yes/no and Who? What? Where? When? questions<br>• Have students label, manipulate, evaluate pictures and objects<br>• Ask questions requiring responses of lists of words<br>• Ask open-ended questions<br>• Ask choice questions, "Do you like____or _____?"<br>• Have students describe personal experiences<br>• Use art and mime<br>• Use four domains of language—Listening, Speaking, Reading, and Writing—at the student's language proficiency level in each domain |

| Bloom's Leveled Verbs | |
|---|---|
| Knowledge | show, point, list |
| Comprehension | identify, recognize, illustrate |
| Application | sketch, construct, build |
| Analysis | diagram |
| Synthesis | arrange, construct, assemble |
| Evaluation | indicate, select |

| EXHIBIT 7.3 | Assessment Matrix Language Acquisition Level 2: Early Production |
|---|---|

| General Description | Students Can | Teacher Should |
|---|---|---|
| Student moves from minimal comprehension and some proficiency in communicating simple ideas to comprehension of highly contextualized information. Student continues to speak in phrases and simple sentences with limited details. Reading and writing progresses with scaffolding and support. | • Reproduce familiar phrases<br>• Speak in simple phrases<br>• Classify or sequence visuals according to oral commands<br>• Match oral reading or stories to illustrations<br>• Simply describe people, places, and things along with more abstract concepts and ideas<br>• Simply retell main events and sequence of a story with some detail<br>• Explain and describe simple academic concepts<br>• Identify in words or simple phrases the "big ideas" and details in content areas<br>• Recognize, read basic vocabulary and write words and simple sentences<br>• Complete or produce sentences from word banks or word walls<br>• Identify basic elements of narratives (characters, setting)<br>• Identify facts from illustrated text<br>• Extend "sentence starters"<br>• Sequence illustrated fiction or nonfiction text<br>• Locate main ideas in simple sentences | • Ask yes/no and Who? What? Where? questions (literal responses)<br>• Encourage expanded responses<br>• Use extended Cloze frames<br>• Ask questions requiring simple comparisons, descriptions, and sequencing of events<br>• Use art and mime<br>• Ask open-ended questions<br>• Ask students to develop story frames<br>• Have students describe personal experiences<br>• Use four domains of language—Listening, Speaking, Reading, and Writing—at the student's language proficiency level in each domain |

| Bloom's Leveled Verbs | |
|---|---|
| Knowledge | show, point, list |
| Comprehension | identify, recognize, illustrate, demonstrate |
| Application | sketch, construct, build, choose, demonstrate |
| Analysis | diagram, classify |
| Synthesis | arrange, construct, assemble, collect |
| Evaluation | indicate, select, choose |

| EXHIBIT 7.4 | Assessment Matrix Language Acquisition Level 3: Speech Emergence |
|---|---|

| General Description | Students Can | Teacher Should |
|---|---|---|
| Student moves from comprehension of contextualized information and proficiency in communicating simple ideas to increased comprehension and communication skills. Student begins to speak in complex sentences with increased details. Reading and writing progresses with scaffolding and support. | • Use context to make more meaning and increased connections to academic understanding<br>• Match oral descriptions or oral readings to illustrations<br>• Answer simple content-based questions orally and in writing using basic sentences<br>• Identify main ideas and some details<br>• Describe events, people, processes, and procedures<br>• Produce simple expository or narrative text<br>• Engage in problem solving<br>• Retell short stories or events<br>• State opinions<br>• Begin to express time through the use of tenses<br>• Give brief, oral content-based presentations<br>• Compare/contrast information, events, and characters<br>• Identify and describe topic sentences, main ideas, and details<br>• Simply summarize story or informational text<br>• Identify with more detail "big ideas" and content-area details<br>• Generate descriptions with increased details<br>• Draw comparisons<br>• Define new vocabulary | • Ask yes/no and Who? What? Where? questions and expect extended responses<br>• Encourage students to describe personal and second-hand experiences<br>• Engage students in making predictions and inferences<br>• Ask students to explain text features such as headings, charts, maps, and graphics<br>• Ask How? and Why? questions as well as open-ended, higher-level thinking questions<br>• Ask students to explain steps in problem solving<br>• Use four domains of language—Listening, Speaking, Reading, and Writing—at the student's language proficiency level in each domain |

| Bloom's Leveled Verbs ||
|---|---|
| Knowledge | name, recall, tell |
| Comprehension | retell, describe, rearrange, predict |
| Application | use, plan |
| Analysis | question, experiment, test, describe |
| Synthesis | write, create, prepare |
| Evaluation | estimate, consider |

| EXHIBIT 7.5 | Assessment Matrix Language Acquisition Level 4: Intermediate Fluency |
|---|---|

| General Description | Students Can | Teacher Should |
|---|---|---|
| Student has very good comprehension of information and near-native proficiency to communicate using both social and academic language. Student has an expanded vocabulary to achieve academically. Student is at or above grade level in reading and writing. | • Comprehend grade-level texts with little support<br>• Use details to make predictions<br>• Organize and generate written compositions based on purpose, audience, and subject matter with little support<br>• Differentiate between fact and opinion in narrative and expository text<br>• Summarize content-based information<br>• Explain strategies used in problem solving<br>• Complete content-related tasks based on information presented orally<br>• Present content-based oral reports<br>• Answer opinion questions with supporting details<br>• Justify ideas<br>• Comprehend, generate discussions and presentations in academic settings<br>• Prepare and deliver presentations/reports across grade-level content areas that use a variety of sources, and include purpose, point of view, transitions, and conclusions | • Ask How? and Why? questions as well as open-ended, higher-order thinking questions<br>• Provide opportunities for student-generated presentations<br>• Provide for a variety of realistic writing opportunities in a variety of genres<br>• Provide increased opportunities for students to use higher-order thinking skills.<br>• Establish opportunities for students to lead group discussions<br>• Ask students to summarize text<br>• Use four domains of language—Listening, Speaking, Reading, and Writing—at the student's language proficiency level in each domain |

### Bloom's Leveled Verbs

| | |
|---|---|
| Knowledge | how, why, retell |
| Comprehension | compare, contrast, predict |
| Application | demonstrate, plan, use |
| Analysis | explain, support, relate |
| Synthesis | propose, compose, design, write |
| Evaluation | value, assess, judge, justify |

| EXHIBIT 7.6 | Assessment Matrix Language Acquisition Level 5: Advanced Fluency | | |
|---|---|---|---|

| General Description | | Students Can | Teacher Should |
|---|---|---|---|
| Student has excellent comprehension of information and near-native proficiency to communicate using both social and academic language. Student has a sophisticated vocabulary, and can respond to figurative language and idiomatic expressions. Student can read fluently and comprehend grade-level texts and content. | | • Distinguish between literal and figurative language in oral discourse<br>• Justify/defend opinions with evidence<br>• Explain in detail the results of inquiry or experiments<br>• Make inferences from text read aloud<br>• Critique material and support argument<br>• Draw conclusions from explicit or implicit grade-level text<br>• Read and comprehend grade-level texts<br>• Make connections between written text and personal experiences<br>• Speak fluently in social and grade-level academic settings<br>• Make detailed predictions<br>• Organize and generate written compositions based on purpose, audience, and subject matter with no support<br>• Connect or integrate personal experiences with literature or content<br>• Defend a point of view<br>• Use figurative language and idiomatic expressions appropriately | • Ask students to summarize information from multiple, related texts<br>• Ask analytical questions about grade-level text<br>• Ask How? and Why? questions as well as open-ended, higher-order thinking questions<br>• Provide for a variety of realistic writing opportunities in a variety of genres<br>• Utilize reading tasks using varied genres<br>• Provide opportunities for peer critiquing, and editing<br>• Provide increased opportunities for students to use higher-order thinking skills<br>• Use four domains of language—Listening, Speaking, Reading, and Writing—at the student's language proficiency level in each domain |
| **Bloom's Leveled Verbs** | | | |
| Knowledge | how, why | | |
| Comprehension | compare, contrast, extend | | |
| Application | consider, test, apply, use | | |
| Analysis | analyze, debate, examine | | |
| Synthesis | formulate, suggest, compose, write | | |
| Evaluation | value, assess, judge, defend, justify | | |

| EXHIBIT 7.7 | Sample Differentiated Assessment and Instruction Blueprint for Grades 3–5 |
| --- | --- |

**Differentiated Assessment Blueprint.**   Content Area: Science (Grades 3–5)

**Scientific Inquiry:** Organize and evaluate observations, measurements, and other data to formulate inferences and conclusions. Develop, design, and safely conduct scientific investigations and communicate the results.

| | Pre-Production | Early Production | Speech Emergence | Intermediate Fluency | Advanced Fluency |
| --- | --- | --- | --- | --- | --- |
| Differentiated Asssessment Tasks | • Complete data collection chart using illustrations on a lab flowchart.<br>• Respond to questions regarding data collected through nonverbal responses (referring to labeled and illustrated lab). | • Complete data collection chart using illustrations accompanied by words and phrases.<br>• Respond to questions by referring to labeled lab using words and phrases. | • Complete data collection chart using complete sentences.<br>• Prepare and deliver a short presentation of findings. | • Complete data collection chart.<br>• Students will write predictions of what they think will happen during the lab, and present their results and conclusions. | • Complete data collection chart.<br>• Students will write predictions of what they think will happen during the lab, and present their results and conclusions. Presentation will include statistics, facts, and comparisons. |

# CONCLUSION

Teachers are feeling more overburdened than ever before. The resources in the preceding section help them take the common formative assessments they are using and differentiate them to meet the needs of English learners, particularly those in the lower levels of language acquisition. The first step is determining whether as a content team or grade level we are truly implementing common formative assessments. The four reflective questions near the beginning of the chapter help teachers determine whether they are on the right track, and if not, how close they are and what steps they can take to get there. The next step is to learn how to take the data collected from these differentiated assessments and use it to make instructional decisions that will ultimately help to meet the needs of all students.

## DISCUSSION QUESTIONS

1. Have I been made aware of the overall language proficiency levels of my English learners?

2. If not, who on my campus can provide that information for me?

3. In addition to an overall language proficiency level, do content or self-contained teachers also receive proficiency levels in each of the four domains: Listening, Speaking, Reading, and Writing?

4. If we say we are currently implementing common formative assessments, does our definition and process match the steps outlined in the four questions near the beginning of this chapter?

5. Can the Assessment Matrices in this chapter help us differentiate our assessments, at a minimum for Level 1 and 2 students?

# CHAPTER 8

# Collaborative Analysis of Assessment Results

While at a recent conference on Professional Learning Communities (PLCs), a term used by one of the presenters had a particularly profound effect on me. When referring to data, the presenter, Rick DuFour, stated that we in education are suffering from D.R.I.P. syndrome; we are Data Rich but Information Poor (DuFour and Eaker, 1998). At a time when everywhere we turn we are being admonished to use data, it bears saying that not all data is created equal. Many of us have, in fact, spent frustratingly numerous hours collecting and analyzing data only to feel just as helpless after our analysis as we did before. The whole purpose of data analysis is to help us pinpoint what we are doing well so that we can replicate it. By the same token, good-quality data can also help us identify what isn't working so that we can cease doing it. If only it were so simple! The secret to any of this happening lies in the quality of the data that we use. If, in fact, we were to use the results of accurate and thoughtfully written common formative assessments, then we could feel confident that the instructional decisions we were making would help our students, particularly our English learners, reach the highest levels of achievement. The information in Chapters 1 through 7 will help us to take the first steps toward making this a reality.

## USING THE RESULTS

The Data Teams process is a six-step process that teachers can use to help make informed instructional decisions. The steps are as follows:

1. **Collect and Chart Data.** Prior to the first Data Team meeting, the team works together to create the common formative pre- or post-assessment and administer it. By the first meeting, teachers have administered the assessment and are ready to analyze the data.

2. **Analyze to Prioritize.** Teachers work together to share the strengths and obstacles of each group of students: those Proficient, Close to Proficient, Far to Go, and those in need of Intensive Intervention. They will use this information to help identify strategies later in Step 4.

3. **Set S.M.A.R.T. Goals.** Based on the performance of each group of students—Proficient, Close, Far to Go, Intensive Intervention—determine a timely, attainable, and relevant goal.

4. **Identify Strategies.** Using the list of strengths and obstacles for each group of students, identify strategies that will have the greatest impact on student achievement. Ensure that all teachers on the team are clear about how the strategies are to be implemented. Remember, implementation matters!

5. **Determine Results Indicators.** Identify the specific student and teacher behaviors that you will see when the strategies are working. I like to think of results indicators as "If ..., then ..." statements.

6. **Monitor Implementation.** Between the administration of the pre- and post-assessments, schedule a time for the team to meet in order to monitor the implementation of strategies. This is a great time to come together as a team just to be sure that all are correctly implementing the agreed-upon strategies. This is also a great time to clarify the strategies for each other as well as discuss whether the team is seeing the expected results indicators. If not, then it may be time for a midcourse correction.

## THE ROLE OF A PROFESSIONAL LEARNING COMMUNITY

I often work with school sites or districts that believe they are implementing Professional Learning Communities. When I get to work with teams of teachers and ask them exactly what that means, most are at a loss for words. What I hear most often is, "Our principal makes us do this, so we fill out the forms she gives us, but really we're just having a grade-level meeting." That statement is often followed by, "Can you tell us what it is?" As mentioned in Chapter 1, I believe that the first order of business with any new initiative is clearly defining it so that all stakeholders understand what it is that is being implemented. For many schools and districts, this never happened. I like to say that a Professional Learning Community is what we are—a team of teachers working together to learn from our students so that we can best serve their needs. As such, we share a common vision, mission, values, and goals. A Data Team is what we do. It is the work of a Professional Learning Community to analyze data and act on that analysis. Let's further define Professional Learning Communities. A true Professional Learning Community is bound by the following four questions.

## Critical Corollary Questions that Drive a PLC

1. **What are students supposed to know and be able to do? (Priority Standards)** This question sounds deceptively simple to answer, but in reality, it is not. It implies that we have identified the priority standards, "unwrapped" them, identified their respective levels of rigor, written Big Ideas and Essential Questions, and defined proficiency.

2. **How do we know when our students have learned? (Common Formative Assessments)** We will know when students have mastered the standard when they have successfully answered the common formative pre- and post-assessment questions. This also implies that we take the time to analyze the results of the assessments so that we can accurately differentiate instruction.

3. **How do we respond when students haven't learned?** *(Intervention)* Once we have identified our strategies, used them to teach the content, then administered our post-assessment, we may find that not all students have learned the content. Teachers use the data to provide targeted intervention that helps students get from where they are to where they need to be.

4. **How do we respond when students already know the content?** *(Differentiation)* If we administer the common formative pre-assessment and find we have students who have clearly mastered the content before we've taught it, how is instruction going to look different for them? This is perhaps one of the most neglected groups in our classrooms today. Sadly, most of our resources go toward helping the struggling students, but as teachers, we need to ensure that we are appropriately differentiating our instruction so that our advanced students can be fully engaged and equipped with the tools to soar to new heights. (DuFour and Eaker, 1998)

These four questions should drive everything that a PLC does. The corollary questions provide structure to the PLC and help clarify the PLC process for teachers.

Whether you call your team a Data Team or a Professional Learning Community is not what matters. Ultimately, it is the work that this team does that makes a difference to the students sitting in our classrooms. Acting upon the data that we have collected is critical to meeting the needs of all students. The Data Teams process helps teams of teachers make sense of data that might otherwise never be used. Exhibit 8.1 illustrates the five steps that take place during a Data Team meeting. The PLC process helps us build the vision, mission, values, and goals that help keep us focused on student achievement.

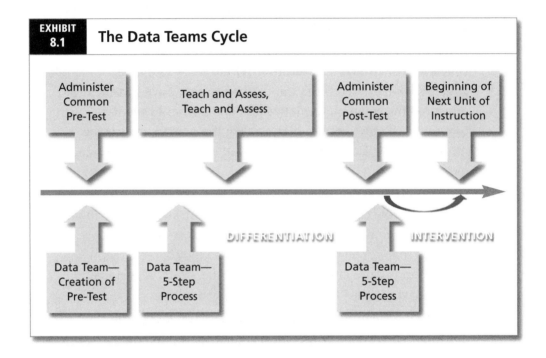

**EXHIBIT 8.1    The Data Teams Cycle**

Administer Common Pre-Test

Teach and Assess, Teach and Assess

Administer Common Post-Test

Beginning of Next Unit of Instruction

DIFFERENTIATION          INTERVENTION

Data Team— Creation of Pre-Test

Data Team— 5-Step Process

Data Team— 5-Step Process

## DATA TEAMS FOR
## ENGLISH LANGUAGE LEARNERS

Let's revisit the six-step Data Teams process with English learners in mind. What we know is that Data Teams can help teachers make instructional decisions for English learners that are based upon data and that help students move from where they are to where they need to be in their learning.

1. **Collect and Chart Data.** Prior to the first meeting of the Data Team, the team works together to differentiate the common formative pre- or post-assessment for English learners. While it would be ideal to differentiate for all five levels of language acquisition, at a minimum the common formative assessment should be differentiated for Levels 1 through 3. Once the assessment has been differentiated, teachers administer it. By the first meeting,

teachers have scored the assessments, analyzed student work by language proficiency level, and are ready to analyze the data.

2. **Analyze to Prioritize.** Teachers work together to share the strengths and obstacles of students in each of the language proficiency levels. English learners are divided into those Proficient, Close to Proficient, Far to Go, and in need of Intensive Intervention. Teachers will use this information to help identify strategies later in Step 4.

3. **Set S.M.A.R.T. Goals.** Based on the performance of English learners in each language proficiency level, teachers identify timely, attainable, and relevant goals for those who are Proficient, Close, Far to Go, and in need of Intensive Intervention.

4. **Identify Strategies.** Using the list of strengths and obstacles for each level of language proficiency, identify strategies that will have the greatest impact on student achievement. Ensure that all teachers on the team are clear about how the strategies are to be implemented. Remember, implementation matters!

5. **Determine Results Indicators.** Identify the specific student and teacher behaviors that you will see when the strategies are working. I like to think of results indicators as "If . . . , then . . ." statements.

6. **Monitor Implementation.** Between the administration of the pre- and post-assessments, schedule a time for the team to meet in order to monitor the implementation of strategies. This is a great time to come together as a team just to be sure that all are correctly implementing the agreed-upon strategies. This is also an opportunity to clarify the strategies for each other as well as discuss whether the team is seeing the expected results indicators. If not, then it may be time for midcourse corrections.

## DIFFERENTIATED INSTRUCTION—HOW TO MEET THE NEEDS OF YOUR ENGLISH LEARNERS

*Differentiated instruction* has now become an overused term in education. In fact, from my conversations with educators around the country, I fear that the term may have lost its meaning. It is one of those terms, like Professional Learning Communities, that was broadly adopted but never clearly defined for those of us on the front lines every day. I clearly remember thinking, "What exactly does that look like?" when my administrator would visit my classroom and later ask me how I was differentiating instruction. My only goal at that point was to ensure that I received a satisfactory evaluation, and so I would proceed with a detailed explanation of what I thought to be differentiated instruction and how I would be applying it in my classroom. Fortunately for me, my definition matched my administrator's. Instead of continuing that trend, let's begin by defining differentiated instruction.

Tracey Hall (2002), senior research scientist at the National Center on Accessing the General Curriculum (NCAC), defined differentiated instruction as "a process to approach teaching and learning for students of differing abilities in the same class. The intent of differentiating instruction is to maximize each student's growth and individual success by meeting each student where he or she is, and assisting in the learning process." She goes on to remind us that three elements of instruction can be differentiated: the content—*what the teacher plans to teach*; the process—*how the teacher plans instruction*; and the product—the *assessment of content.* Throughout this book, you have been equipped with the tools necessary to differentiate the product, or assessment, for English learners. Using the information from a well-differentiated assessment is an integral first step in differentiating the content or process for your English learners.

After the administration of the differentiated pre-assessment, the Data Teams process will help you determine the students who fall into the following categories:

1. Already proficient

2. Close to Proficient

3. Far to Go

4. In need of Intensive Support

Analyzing each of these four groups helps teachers pinpoint areas of strength and weakness. Armed with this level of clarity about where their students are in relation to the learning target not only provides excellent feedback to students, but also provides a road map for teachers to follow to help their students meet proficiency.

## GRADING ENGLISH LANGUAGE LEARNERS

Grading is one of the most controversial subjects in education. Research has shown that there are many reasons for this, but considering the current environment of accountability, I believe that one of the main reasons is that it is one of the last areas in which teachers feel they have some semblance of control. While we like to believe that grades are the one true objective measure of success or failure in the classroom, there has been much research to the contrary. In fact, such experts in the field as Ken O'Connor (2010) and Douglas Reeves (2011) have made it clear that despite what we'd like to believe, grades are anything but objective. Even in this era of standards, grades on those standards are often influenced by elements wholly unrelated to mastery of the standards. Issues about grading can only be resolved if we have clarity of purpose. Here are some questions that schools and districts need to grapple with when it comes to grading ELLs:

1. What purpose do grades serve?

2. If the purpose is communication, then does our current grading policy allow teachers to communicate accurately the progress that ELLs are making in
   • English language acquisition?
   • Core content areas: Reading, Math, History, Science?

3. If the answer to question 2 is no, what first steps can we take to change that?

Unfortunately, it has been determined by research study after research study that grades are more a measure of a teacher's opinion of a student than a true reflection of what the student knows and is able to do (Reeves, 2011). This has tremendous implications for English learners when teachers assign failing grades year after year because these students are not proficient in English and most have therefore not met the standards. For those who have graded English learners in this way, I would like to pose a simple question: If English learners receive failing grades year after year, despite any progress they may have made in their language proficiency, how do we suppose their motivation has been affected? If I had been reminded time and again of my failure, I would certainly begin to believe that I was, in fact, a failure.

## THE ALTERNATIVE

One alternative to issuing a continuous stream of failing grades is to create a differentiated grade report that is sent home along with the regular report card. In this supplemental report, the parents and the student are made aware of the student's progress in language proficiency. If, for example, the student has progressed from a Level 2 in Reading to a Level 3, then the parents and student are made aware of this progress. Not only does this reinforce the student's awareness of the growth he has made in a specific domain, it also inspires hope in him. It confirms for him that although he may not have reached proficiency on the state standards, he has certainly made progress in his acquisition of the English language. This information may prevent some English learners from losing hope, dropping out of school, and becoming statistics.

# CONCLUSION

Teacher collaboration has in recent years become the expected way of functioning at schools and districts throughout the country. No longer is it acceptable or even wise for teachers to work in isolation. Collaborative structures such as PLCs and Data Teams abound, but the bottom line of any structure, strategy, or initiative should ultimately be student achievement. In this case, teams of teachers working collaboratively to design and analyze the results of common formative assessments is a vital piece of the puzzle when it comes to educating English learners. Is it possible for teachers to accomplish these tasks alone? The answer is yes—with hours of personal and professional time dedicated to the cause, it is indeed possible for a lone teacher to accomplish what has been proposed in this book. However, if the question is whether it is effective for teachers to try to accomplish these tasks alone, the answer is most certainly a resounding no. Research has shown that we do our best work when we collaborate and that it is in that collaborative environment that teachers often thrive, never again returning to the days of working in solitude and isolation. When striving to help English learners attain rigorous standards of learning, it is a necessity to work with our colleagues.

When we become a Professional Learning Community, we work toward a common goal, ensuring that all students learn. While a PLC may be what we are and while a Data Team may be what we do, we sometimes struggle to know how to use the data we have mined from our common formative assessments. This chapter has taught us a process we can use to analyze the data and make instructional decisions that will result in greater learning for English learners. Chapter 9 will delineate the steps we can take to implement and sustain common formative assessments for English learners.

# DISCUSSION QUESTIONS

1. How does our school/district encourage collaboration among teachers? Has collaboration become the way we do business?

2. Do all teachers define collaboration the same way? If we are implementing PLCs, do the four corollary questions listed in this chapter drive all the work that we do? When we meet as a PLC, are we consistently meeting around one of those four questions?

3. Do we have a data analysis protocol in place to help teams of teachers analyze data? More importantly, does the data analysis protocol end in action? In other words, do we stop at data analysis, or do we act upon the data to improve student achievement?

# CHAPTER 9

# Implementing and Sustaining Powerful Practices for English Learners

Access to a "guaranteed and viable curriculum" (Marzano, 2003) should be a minimal expectation for all students. If this were indeed so, it would mean a significant increase in excellence and equity for many ELLs. Sadly, a large number of English learners across the nation are not provided with equal access to a common curriculum. Before students are held accountable for meeting educational standards, schools should be held accountable for giving all students the opportunity to learn the full scope of what is tested or measured (LaCelle-Peterson and Rivera, 1994). While Chapters 1 through 8 have provided a road map for teachers to follow to begin to put this basic expectation in place, this chapter provides some ideas and suggestions for ensuring that it truly becomes a reality at your school or district.

## GETTING STARTED

The first step in beginning any process is taking stock of where you currently are in the process as a school or district. I would begin by simply identifying where you are in relation to implementing common formative assessments for all students. The series of questions that follow will help your team determine whether you are truly implementing common formative assessments or if instead you are simply using "assessments in common."

1. Did we begin by identifying priority standards for our content area? Did we use the following criteria to identify the priorities?

   **Endurance (Life):** Is this standard a life skill that students will use in their everyday lives?

   **Leverage (Test):** Is this standard assessed on the state language proficiency assessment?

   **Readiness (School):** Is this standard a prerequisite skill for language learning that will take place in school in years to come?

2. Did we "unwrap" the standard(s) into the component concepts and skills along with Bloom's Taxonomy levels?

3. Did we take into consideration the purpose for our assessment? Is it meant to take place at the end of learning to help us determine whether our students have met the standard(s) (**summative assessment**)? Is it meant to take place while the learning is happening to help us provide formative feedback to our students so that they can see the gap between where they are and where they need to be, as well as the steps they can take to close the gap (**formative assessment**)? Will the results provide feedback to us that will help us refine, adjust, and focus our instruction?

4. Will we use Data Teams or another data analysis protocol to analyze the results of the assessment? Will the analysis process involve identifying where each student is in relation to the target and then identifying the research-based strategies that will help him reach the target?

As explained in Chapter 7, if your team has answered in the positive to all four questions, then you are most certainly implementing common formative assessments. If not, then the first step is assessing exactly where you are in the process. If your team has not answered yes to a single one of the questions, then the fact that you are reading this book counts as a first step toward implementation.

When implementing common formative assessments, keep in mind the research by Douglas Reeves that confirms that the degree of implementation matters. Implementing an initiative half-heartedly not only did not result in scores that were better than when the initiative was not implemented at all, but in some cases actually had a negative effect on achievement (Reeves, 2010). It is therefore in our best interests and in that of our students to ensure that we are implementing a strategy to the deepest level possible. Following are some questions to consider:

1. How much do our teachers know and understand about creating common formative assessments?

2. Do we presently have the resources to implement common formative assessments school-/district-wide? If not, is there a team or school that may be willing to move forward with this initiative?

3. What type of professional development can we offer teachers who are interested in implementing?

4. Do we have a measure for assessing language proficiency periodically throughout the year? Is the state language proficiency assessment the only measure we have in place?

5. Once we have begun work on our common formative assessments, how can we assist content-area teachers in differentiating the assessments, particularly for English learners in the lowest levels of language proficiency?

The responses to these initial five questions will help an ESL, content, or school team determine whether they are ready to begin the process.

## IMPLEMENTATION GUIDE

Once we understand where we are in the process and know what resources we have at our disposal, it is important for leaders to convey a vision of an aligned standards, instruction, and assessment system. When everyone understands the alignment described in Chapters 1 through 3, they are less apt to see each element as a separate initiative and instead will understand that each element plays a part in the big picture (see the alignment diagram in Exhibit 3.2). For example, aligned assessments can't exist without a clear and coherent curriculum. One depends upon the other. Once teachers understand how all these pieces fit together, they will be more likely to be open to the idea of implementation. If, instead, educators see each element of common formative assessments as a separate and distinct element, occurring in isolation from everything else they do, then it is likely to be perceived as "one more disconnected initiative with no hope of survival." We saw in Chapter 1 that common formative assessments of language proficiency and content are essential if we are to turn the tide of achievement for English learners. Helping educators understand the role they play in the bigger picture is a necessary step in the process.

As Ainsworth and Viegut (2006) remind us, the deep and effective implementation of common formative assessments requires "high expectations with high support for the educators doing the actual implementation" (p. 111). Going on to describe what this would look like, they reiterate that educators cannot have a full plate of initiatives to implement if any one of them is to stand a chance. Michael Fullan (2001) accurately refers to the incessant addition of new initiatives to the already full plates of educators as a "disturbance": "Taking all the innovations that come along is not the kind of disturbance that is going to approximate any desired outcome" (p. 109).

Leaders must then provide focus for their teaching staff. A great way to begin to do this is to take stock of all the initiatives that are currently being implemented. Then, carefully and honestly gauge the impact that each is having on instruction. If you cannot gauge the impact definitively, then how have you been keeping track of this initiative to begin with? Any worthwhile initiative should be accompanied by a rigorous data and accountability system so that at any point in time the question "Is the initiative working?" can be clearly answered.

If common formative assessments are to stand a chance, they will require a deep investment of time, energy, and resources. Demonstrating to your staff that you are committed to this endeavor, then backing up that commitment with a promise for focus will go a long way toward moving this initiative forward. In my experience, I have found that teachers are not afraid of work; rather they resent expending countless hours, resources, and energy on an initiative that is abandoned as quickly as it was adopted. "If leaders (1) hold to these high expectations; (2) provide the high support needed to the educators carrying out the implementation; and (3) doggedly maintain this as a priority ... then common formative assessments are sure to become part of the instructional culture of the school and district" (Ainsworth and Viegut, 2006, p. 112).

## TAKING STOCK

It is important to realize at the beginning of this implementation that, like any change, it will be fraught with challenges. If we are prepared for those challenges, then the initiative stands a better chance of becoming integrated into the school/district culture. It is also important to accept that change is not an event but rather a process, and that if we are to be successful at changing practice, then we need to be prepared to settle in for the long haul. Some estimates put any meaningful change at three to five years for full implementation. Some are frustrated by that figure and often respond with, "But we don't have three to five years!" My response is simple— there is no time like the present! If we sit on the sidelines lamenting the fact that we don't have time, then we squander the little time we do have with inaction. If we can commit to doing it and doing it right, then we embark on a journey that will end with improved achievement for all students in our school or district. What are we waiting for?

The first step in implementing any new initiative is to take stock of where you are as a school/district or staff.

1. Do we have a clear vision of where we want to be?

2. Do we have the resources and supports in place to help us achieve our vision?

3. Do we have a clear process in place to guide our staff through the implementation process? Do we know what we need to do first, next?

4. Are there currently other initiatives being implemented?

5. How is the teaching staff feeling about those initiatives? Have we been able to remove any that are not working?

6. Does the staff perceive this as an area of need? If not, what information/data can I share that will help them feel the sense of urgency?

7. Do I have district support for this initiative? Board of education support? Support from the teachers union? If not, how can I build support for this initiative?

8. Is the budget dedicated toward staff and curriculum development sufficient to support the implementation? What about Title I or Title III funds?

9. Have we allotted a sufficient amount of time to allow for effective implementation?

10. What possible hurdles are we anticipating? How will we address those hurdles when they arise?

11. Will I be able to maintain a sustained focus on implementation over the next year? Two years? Three years? Five years? (Adapted from Ainsworth and Viegut, 2006, pp. 125–126)

Once these questions have been explored and addressed in depth, it is important to use the information gleaned to craft an implementation plan. The plan should consist of five columns: Current State, Desired State, Action Steps, Responsible Party, and Time Frame (see Exhibit 9.1). Once armed with an implementation plan, it is important to take the next step and commit to it by adding dates for completion as well as persons responsible. This will help to ensure that your plan goes beyond good intentions.

| EXHIBIT 9.1 | Implementation Plan | | | |
|---|---|---|---|---|
| **Current State** | **Desired State** | **Action Steps to Get There** | **Responsible Party** | **Time Frame** |
| | | | | |

# CONCLUSION

I remember as a child complaining whenever I knew any homework assignment would take a significant amount of time. My father would always remind me that anything worthwhile always takes time. Never has that statement had more meaning than when implementing common formative assessments. We know from the research that, as a strategy, formative assessment and the feedback it yields have among the highest effect sizes on student achievement. Therefore, we know that implementing common formative assessments is worthwhile indeed. All that is left is the will and courage to make it happen to turn the tide of achievement for every English learner who walks through our doors.

## DISCUSSION QUESTIONS

1. Where are we currently in the process of implementing an integrated system of curriculum, instruction, and assessment? Do we have the support we need to advance our implementation?

2. How committed is our staff to the idea of assessing English learners effectively through the use of collaboratively written common formative assessments?

3. After completing the inventory of 11 questions in the Taking Stock section of this chapter, what have we found to be the level of commitment from our site administration? District administration? Board of education? Teachers union? How can we work together to build a shared vision of equitable assessment for all students?

4. Will the implementation plan be completed for our whole school? Or will we proceed with one grade level or content area for the first year of implementation? How can we use that first year to help us further our vision of equitable assessment?

# References

Abedi, J. (2007). *English language proficiency assessment in the nation: Current status and future practice.* Davis, CA: Regents of the University of California, Davis.

Abedi, J. (2008). Classification system for English language learners. *Educational Measurement: Issues and Practice, 27*(3), 17–31.

Abedi, J., & Dietel, R. (2004). *Challenges in the No Child Left Behind Act for English language learners.* (CRESST Policy Brief No. 7). Los Angeles, CA: National Center for Research on Evaluation, Standards and Student Testing. http://www.cse.ucla.edu/products/policy/cresst_policy7.pdf (accessed February 20, 2010).

Abedi, J., & Lord, C. (2001). The language factor in mathematics tests. *Applied Measurement in Education, 14,* 219–234.

Ainsworth, L. (2003). *Priority standards.* Englewood, CO: Lead + Learn Press.

Ainsworth, L., & Viegut, D. (2006). *Common formative assessments: How to connect standards-based instruction and assessment.* Thousand Oaks, CA: Corwin Press.

Bachman, L. F., Bailey, A. L., Griffin, N., Herman, J. L., & Wolf, M. K. (2008). *Recommendations for assessing English language learners: English language proficiency measures and accommodation uses.* Los Angeles, CA: UCLA, National Center for Research on Evaluation, Standards and Student Testing (CRESST). http://www.cse.ucla.edu/products/reports/R737.pdf (accessed March 13, 2011).

Bishop, B. (2010). *Accelerating academic achievement for English language learners* (training manual). Englewood, CO: Lead + Learn Press.

Bracey, G. (2004). Value-added assessment findings: Poor kids get poor teachers. *Phi Delta Kappan, 86*(4), 331–333.

Capps, R., Fix, M., Murray, J., Ost, J., Passel, J. S., & Herwantoro, S. (2005). *The new demography of America's schools: Immigration and the No Child Left Behind Act.* Washington, DC: The Urban Institute. http://www.urban.org/UploadedPDF/311230_new_demography.pdf (accessed November 26, 2010).

Capps, R., Fix, M., Ost, J., Reardon-Anderson, J., & Passel, J. (2004). *The health and well-being of young children of immigrants.* New York, NY: Urban Institute.

Cochran-Smith, M., & Zeichner, K. (2006). *Studying teacher education: The report of the American Education Research Association Panel on research and teacher education.* Washington, D.C.: AERA.

Colvin, R., & Johnson, J. (2007). Know the game and cover the action. *Education Week, 27*(19), 36.

Conley, D. (2005). *College knowledge: What it really takes for students to succeed and how we can get them ready.* San Francisco, CA: Jossey-Bass.

Cummins, J. (1996). *Negotiating identities: Education for empowerment in a diverse society.* Los Angeles, CA: California Association for Bilingual Education.

Cummins, R. (1989). *Meaning and mental representation.* Cambridge, MA: MIT Press.

De Cohen, C., Clemencia, N. D., & Clewell, B. C. (2005). *Profile of U.S. elementary schools: LEP concentration and school capacity.* Washington, DC: Urban Institute.

DuFour, R., & Eaker, R. (1998). *Professional learning communities at work: Best practices for enhancing student achievement.* Bloomington, IN: National Education Service.

Espinosa, L., Laffey, J., & Whittaker, T. (2006). *Language minority children analysis: Focus on technology use.* Los Angeles, CA: CRESST/NCES.

Fullan, M. (2001). *Leading in a culture of change.* San Francisco, CA: Jossey-Bass.

Gándara, P., Maxwell-Jolly, J., & Driscoll, A. (2005). *Listening to teachers of English Learners.* Santa Cruz, CA: Center for the Future of Teaching and Learning. http://lmri.ucsb.edu/publications/05_listening-to-teachers.pdf (accessed May 7, 2011).

Hall, T. (2002). *Differentiated instruction: Effective classroom practices report.* Washington, DC: National Center on Accessing the General Curriculum.

Hattie, J. (2009). *Visible learning. A synthesis of over 800 meta-analyses relating to achievement.* New York, NY: Routledge.

Hill, J. D., & Flynn, K. M. (2006). *Classroom instruction that works with English language learners.* Alexandria, VA: Association for Supervision and Curriculum Development.

Krashen, S. D. (1981). *Second language acquisition and second language learning.* Elmsford, NY: Pergamon Press.

Krashen, S., & Terrell, T. (1983). *The natural approach: Language acquisition in the classroom.* Hayward, CA: Alemany Press.

LaCelle-Peterson, M., & Rivera, C. (1994). Is it real for all kids? A framework for equitable assessment policies for English language learners. *Harvard Educational Review, 64*(1), 55–75.

MacSwan, J., & Rolstad, K. (2006). How language proficiency tests mislead us about ability: Implications for English language learners placement in special education. *Teachers College Record, 108*(11), 2304–2328.

Marzano, R. J. (2003). *What works in schools: Translating research into action.* Alexandria, VA: ASCD.

McLaughlin, B. (1992). *Myths and misconceptions about second language learning: What every teacher needs to unlearn.* Santa Cruz, CA: University of California, Santa Cruz, National Center for Research on Cultural Diversity and Second Language Learning.

McLaughlin, B., Blanchard, A., & Osanai, Y. (1995). *Assessing language development in bilingual preschool children.* Washington, DC: George Washington University.

O'Connor, K. (2010). *A repair kit for grading: 15 fixes for broken grades.* Boston, MA: Pearson.

Odden, A. (2009). We know how to turn schools around—we just haven't done it. *Education Week, 29*(14), 22–23.

Popham, J. (2003). *Test better, teach better: The instructional role of assessment.* Alexandria, VA: Association for Supervision and Curriculum Development.

Popham, J. (2008). *Transformative assessment in action: An inside look at applying the process.* Alexandria, VA: Association for Supervision and Curriculum Development.

Ramírez, J., Yuen, S., Ramey, D., & Pasta, D. (1991). *Final report: Longitudinal study of structured English immersion strategy, early-exit and late-exit transitional bilingual education programs for language-minority children* (Vol. I). (Prepared for U.S. Department of Education). San Mateo, CA: Aguirre International.

Reeves, D. B. (2004). *Accountability in action.* 2nd ed. Englewood, CO: Lead + Learn Press.

Reeves, D. B. (2010). *Transforming professional development into student results.* Alexandria, VA: Association for Supervision and Curriculum Development.

Reeves, D. B. (2011). *Elements of grading: A guide to effective practice.* Bloomington, IN: Solution Tree.

Reyes, I., & Moll, L. (2004). Latinos and bilingualism. In *Encyclopedia Latina.* New York, NY: Grolier.

Ruíz-de-Velasco, J., & Fix, M. E. (2000). *Overlooked and underserved: Immigrant students in U.S. secondary schools.* Washington, DC: Urban Institute.

Sanders, W. L., & Horn S. P. (1994). The Tennessee value-added assessment system. *Journal of Personnel Evaluation in Education, 8*(3), 299–311.

Schmoker, M. (2011). *Focus: Elevating the essentials to radically improve student learning.* Alexandria, VA: Association for Supervision and Curriculum Development.

Short, D. J., & Fitzsimmons, S. (2007). *Double the work: Challenges and solutions to acquiring language and academic literacy for adolescent English language learners.* New York, NY: Carnegie Corporation.

Stiggins, R., Arter, J., Chappuis, J., & Chappuis, S. (2005). *Assessment for learning: An action guide for school leaders.* Portland, OR: Assessment Training Institute.

Tabors, P. O. (1997). *One child, two languages: A guide for preschool educators of children learning English as a second language.* Baltimore, MD: Paul H. Brookes.

Thomas, W. P., & Collier, V. P. (1997). School effectiveness for language minority students. *National Clearinghouse for Bilingual Education (NCBE) Resource Collection Series,* No. 9. http://www.thomasandcollier.com/Downloads/1997_Thomas-Collier97.pdf (accessed August 13, 2010).

Thomas, W. P., & Collier, V. P. (2002). *A national study of school effectiveness for language minority students' long-term academic achievement.* Berkeley, CA: University of California, Center for Research on Education, Diversity and Excellence. http://escholarship.ucop.edu/uc/item/65j213pt (accessed March 3, 2011).

# Index